School, Home, Community

You and Your Health
Teacher's Edition

Julius B. Richmond, M.D.
Elenore T. Pounds, M.A.

In consultation with
Orvis A. Harrelson, M.D., M.P.H.
Gladys Gardner Jenkins, M.A.
Dieter H. Sussdorf, Ph.D.
Wallace Ann Wesley, Hs.D.

Scott, Foresman and Company
Glenview, Illinois

Dallas, Texas Palo Alto, California
Oakland, New Jersey Tucker, Georgia

Highlights of *You and Your Health*

A deeply human approach	Opening chapter in each text centers on mental health. Program emphasizes building of positive self-concepts; helps students understand themselves and others.
Easy for students to read and use	High-interest content, effective writing styles, and powerful visuals enhance readability. Readability is at or below grade level according to Fry and Dale-Chall formulas. Anatomical drawings are accurately done by a professional medical illustrator.
Easy to teach	Chapters organized for easy teaching and learning. Helpful "Teacher's Notes" printed on pupil's pages in *Teacher's Edition.* Chapters can be taught in any order. Books can be used with large or small groups or by individuals. Behavioral objectives are posed directly to students. Testing program is built into books. End-of-Book test is action-oriented.
Learner verified	Scott, Foresman health materials have been widely used in the classroom. This new Program has evolved out of 30 years of interaction among learners, teachers, and the publisher. New materials have been classroom tested. Classroom teachers have served as advisors on the Program.
Unique provisions for school-home communication	School and Home feature at the end of each chapter. Supplementary school/home *Activity Booklets* with parents' message on the back of each Activity Sheet.
Age-appropriate content written by health science experts	Content based on research about children's health and safety needs and concerns. Double-checked for accuracy by experts in all areas of the health sciences.

ISBN: 0-673-11013-3

2345678910-RRC-858483828180797877776

Criteria for Selection of a Health Textbook*

Does Level Four cover concepts in those aspects of a complete health education program that are appropriate to nine- to ten-year-olds?

Mental Health, Human Relations, and Values Awareness	*Pages 8–35*
Personal Health, Fitness, and Dental Health	*Pages 98–113, 122–151*
The Body, Human Growth and Development	*Pages 36–69, 116–121*
Nutrition	*Pages 101–107, 122–123*
Family Health	*Pages 35, 69, 97, 103, 106–107, 127, 151, 163–167, 173, 207*
Prevention and Control of Disease, Health Services	*Pages 65, 115, 152–173*
Drugs (Including Alcohol and Tobacco)	*Pages 22–24, 90–92, 115, 161–162*
Community and Environmental Health (Human Ecology)	*Pages 174–207*
Consumer Health	*Pages 92, 178–179, 183, 196–197*
Safety and First Aid	*Pages 70–97*
Health Career Awareness	*Pages 142–145, 163, 177–179*

A guide to the Scope and Teaching Sequence of YOU AND YOUR HEALTH K-8 is available on request from Scott, Foresman and Company. This guide includes concepts and selected behavioral objectives.

Does it motivate children to apply what they are learning in health to their daily lives at school, at home, and in the community?
Pages 15–20, 22–26, 72–97, 101–127, 137–139, 163–167, 174–207

Does it present materials and approaches that include the family in the health education program?
Pages 35, 69, 97, 106–107, 127, 151, 163–165, 173, 183, 188–190, 196–203, 207

Does it use the problem-solving approach to develop critical thinking and decision-making skills on the part of children?
Pages 15–20, 22–26, 73–80, 87–92, 102–103, 108–109

Does it build positive mental-health attitudes in children by enhancing their self-images and fostering appreciation of individual differences?
Pages 8–35, 39, 116–121

---

*Based on Joint Committee on Health Problems in Education of the NEA and the AMA, *Why Health Education in Your School?* and *Suggested School Health Policies*, 5th ed., AMA.

Authors

Consultants

Julius B. Richmond, M.D. Professor of Child Psychiatry and Human Development and Professor and Chairman, Department of Social and Preventive Medicine, Harvard Medical School; Director, Judge Baker Guidance Center; Chief of Psychiatric Service, Children's Hospital Medical Center, Boston, Massachusetts.

Elenore T. Pounds, M.A. Writer; lecturer; former Directing Editor of the Health and Personal Development Program; classroom teacher; coauthor of the *Health and Growth* Program; author of *Drugs and Your Safety* and other *Health Enrichment Booklets.*

Orvis A. Harrelson, M.D., M.P.H. Corporate Medical Director, Weyerhauser Company, Tacoma, Washington; former Administrative Director of Health, Tacoma Public Schools, Tacoma, Washington.

Gladys Gardner Jenkins, M.A. Lecturer in Parent-Child-Teacher Relationships, University of Iowa, Iowa City, Iowa; former member, National Advisory Council on Child Growth and Human Development; author of *Helping Children Reach Their Potential;* coauthor of *These Are Your Children.*

Dieter H. Sussdorf, Ph.D. Associate Professor of Microbiology, Cornell University Graduate School of Medical Sciences, New York, New York; coauthor of *Methods in Immunology.*

Wallace Ann Wesley, Hs.D. Director, Department of Health Education, American Medical Association, Chicago, Illinois; former teacher at primary through college levels.

Learner Feedback

Experimental versions of many of the lessons in YOU AND YOUR HEALTH for grade four were used during the 1975–1976 school year with students at Fern-Greenwood Elementary School, Torrance, California; Ruth N. Upson Elementary School, Jacksonville, Florida; and Public School 276, Brooklyn, New York. The authors and editors of the program are grateful to the students and to the teachers in these schools for their comments and their suggestions.

T4

Content Specialists

 Richard H. Blum, Ph.D. Consulting Professor, Department of Psychology and Director, Joint Program in Drugs, Crime, and Community Studies, Center for Interdisciplinary Research, Stanford University, Stanford, California.

 Norman H. Olsen, D.D.S. Chairman of the Department of Pedodontics and Dean of The Dental School, Northwestern University, Chicago, Illinois.

 Willie D. Ford, Ph.D. Professor, Nutrition and Home Economics, Grambling State University, Grambling, Louisiana; former Nutrition Specialist, U.S. Department of Agriculture, University of Nebraska, Lincoln, Nebraska.

 Marguerite Robinson, M.S. Consumer Specialist, Department of Health, Education, Welfare, Food and Drug Administration, Chicago, Illinois; Past President, Chicago Nutrition Association, Chicago, Illinois.

 Lucia Guzman, B.S. Assistant to the Dean for Student Affairs, University of Texas School of Allied Health Sciences, University of Texas Medical Branch, Galveston, Texas.

 Joan Tillotson, Ph.D. Consultant in Movement Education, The University of North Carolina at Charlotte, Charlotte, North Carolina.

 Barbara J. Kohuth, B.S. Environmental Health Educator; Head, Office of Environmental Education and Public Information, Cleveland Department of Public Health and Welfare, Cleveland, Ohio.

 Wilma Yee, B.S., R.N. Public Health Nurse and School Nurse, Oakland Public Schools, Oakland, California.

 Boyd T. Marsh, M.A., Deputy Health Commissioner for Environmental Health, Cleveland Department of Public Health and Welfare, Cleveland, Ohio.

The assistance of the National Safety Council, Chicago, Illinois, in reviewing the safety advice in this material is gratefully acknowledged.

Contents

Components of Level Four

Program Materials

Pupil's Text

Centers around the special health and safety needs and interests of the nine- to ten-year-old child.

The amount of written material and the reading level are appropriate to fourth-grade readers.

Heavily illustrated including full color photographs, original art, and reproductions of famous masterpieces.

Teacher's Edition

This *Teacher's Edition* contains the following aids:

Teacher's Supplement containing brief, professional "refresher" articles (T11–T24); enrichment suggestions for teaching each lesson (T25–T38); and reference materials for teachers, parents, and pupils (T39–T45). The complete contents are listed on page T6.

Instant-help "Teacher's Notes" in blue in the upper margins of the pupil's pages plus answers to test questions inserted in place.

Supplementary Materials

Activity Booklet

Perforated sheets in this 32-page, consumable booklet have health activities for *school use* on one side, health activities for *home use* and a special health message for parents on the other.

Features of Level Four

Chapter Openers

Each chapter begins with a distinctive introduction which conveys the meaning of the content and poses questions designed to lead the student into the chapter.

Decision-Making Pages

Students are given the opportunity to make decisions about the right thing to do in the areas of mental health and safety. A problem situation is shown in an illustration. Students are asked what they should do in that situation. Then they are told to turn the page. When they turn the page, students find the correct things to do in the situation shown.

Photographic Essays

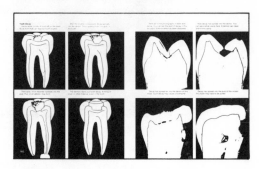

Picture essays are used to give students a look inside the human body, to describe some dangerous places to play, to demonstrate proper tooth-care, and to show them community health workers and problems.

Enrichment Activities

Health- and safety-related poems, riddles, short essays and written reports, and works of art are used throughout the text. "Enjoy It" pages expose the student to health-related poetry and fine art. "Write It" pages provide students with a pleasant way to express themselves, as well as with an opportunity to do some research to expand their understanding of the subject matter.

Health Around Us

The "Health Around Us" page appears throughout the book. It is used to make students aware of intriguing aspects of health and safety in the world around them and to highlight new developments in the field of health.

Chapter Tests

End-of-chapter test is based on the content of the chapter. The test requires the student to choose the correct answer, supply the word to fill in a blank, and/or rewrite false statements on a true-false test to make them true. End-of-book test is action-oriented.

Can You Show What You Know?

This is one of several evaluative techniques used in YOU AND YOUR HEALTH. Here behavioral objectives in the cognitive area are posed to students in simple terms. Students, in turn, give evidence of what they have learned by *observable behavior*.

School and Home

The "School and Home" page is the last page of each chapter in the pupil's text. This page suggests ways the student can bring home newly acquired health knowledge in order to share that knowledge with family members and to incorporate it in daily life.

Learner Feedback

YOU AND YOUR HEALTH has been developed as a result of reactions and suggestions from students and teachers who used the popular HEALTH AND GROWTH Program. Feedback from students and teachers was obtained through questionnaires, correspondence, prepublication testing, and classroom observation.

Level Four of YOU AND YOUR HEALTH contains less written material than level four of the preceding series. The reading level of the new text is on target for the grade level and an especially readable type face has been used.

The content of this text has been reorganized to emphasize cooperation between the school, the home, and the community. The opening chapter is oriented toward building positive self-images and improving students' relationships with each other and with the members of their families. The closing chapter of the text brings the student in contact with community and environmental health problems.

A "School and Home" page at the end of each chapter in YOU AND YOUR HEALTH suggests ways for the child to *bring home* the health knowledge that he or she has gained in that chapter. In addition, a new product—a *School/Home Activity Booklet*—has been made available for use with the text. This consumable booklet is designed to reinforce concepts taught in the text. Each lesson consists of an activity to be done in school, an activity to be done at home, and a health message for parents.

Other features have been included to increase student involvement and awareness of health and safety in their daily living and in the world around them. These include health poems; famous works of art pertaining to some aspect of the subject matter; riddles, puzzles, and short written reports; and articles on interesting health and safety topics.

Finally, the teachability of the Program has been enhanced. A "Preview It" page at the beginning of each chapter introduces the students to the content and organization of the material to follow. And a "Review It" page at the end of each chapter provides students with an opportunity to test their understanding of the material presented. Behavioral objectives, stated in terms the students can understand, are presented as part of each chapter in YOU AND YOUR HEALTH. End-of-chapter tests are designed to test these objectives.

In order to continue Scott, Foresman's practice of making our programs responsive to the needs of students and teachers, we have included learner-feedback questionnaires in the Teacher's Supplement. *We would appreciate your completing the teacher's questionnaire on pages T47 and T48 and returning it to us after you have taught YOU AND YOUR HEALTH for most of the school year. If you would be willing to have your students fill out questionnaires, please make enough copies of the student questionnaire on page T46 for them. Then return the completed questionnaires to Scott, Foresman.*

A Healthful Classroom Environment

If health education is to be effective, it is important that it take place in a classroom environment that is physically and mentally healthy. Here are some things you can do to create a favorable *physical environment* for children.

To create a favorable physical environment
Turn on lights on dark days and try to have chairs and desks or tables arranged so no one faces a strong light or glare.

See that children have chairs and desks that are properly adjusted to their heights.

Allow plenty of time for, and give reminders about washing hands *before* eating and *after* using the toilet.

Alternate periods of concentrated work with periods of relaxing activities; alternate periods of strenuous play with quiet ones.

See that playtimes are a mixture of undirected play and of supervised activity during which pupils may explore and practice such skills as climbing, running, and jumping.

Be aware of the needs of some children for more sleep and adequate food. Tired, hungry children do not learn.

Be alert to signs and complaints of illness—watch for change in skin color (which may indicate fever), skin eruptions, dull or watery eyes, general or unusual listlessness, irritability, signs of a cold. (See "Signs and Symptoms of Illness" on page T13.)

Cooperate with others in the school system in setting up a plan for health examinations and for keeping cumulative health records.

Pay attention to the environment in general —including aesthetics—as influencing the learning process.

The classroom environment which promotes mental health is one in which each child is helped to develop a strong, positive self-image; a feeling of belonging; and a sense of worth. Here are some things you can do to create such an environment.

To foster a strong, positive self-image
Make a point of learning children's names as soon as possible; check with each child to see if there is a nickname he or she prefers.

Encourage the making of self-portraits. If possible, have pupils use hand mirrors to study carefully hair color, eye color, and so on.

Post *all* the children's self-portraits in the classroom. If there isn't room, display them in "shifts" in randomly chosen order or find room in the hall outside the classroom. Be sure portraits are labeled so the child's name can be seen.

Take time for youngsters to talk about the topic "What I Like About Myself." Let them draw pictures of themselves in activities they feel they do well.

Read poems, such as the one in Chapter One, that stress each child's uniqueness.

Look for opportunities to emphasize that each youngster is different in many ways from any other human being; that he or she is "special"; that differences among individuals are natural and to be expected.

Ask children to draw pictures and write simple stories about their homes, their families, their pets, the foods they like best, things they like to do, a time when they felt sad or happy or angry.

To foster a feeling of "belonging"

Make your classroom a warm, friendly place.

Make it a point to celebrate birthdays by establishing simple ceremonies such as singing to the birthday child.

Watch out for the friendless child; do what you can to seat him or her beside outgoing youngsters and to team him or her with friendly children on committees.

When children are absent for a time, call their homes to inquire about their health. Have the class or individuals prepare simple get-well messages. Welcome back the absentees and let pupils brief them on what has happened at school during their absence.

Make special efforts to help newcomers feel comfortable. Assign friendly children to be "Big Brothers" or "Big Sisters" until the newcomers feel at home.

Let boys and girls have a part in planning various class undertakings.

Encourage the children to talk over problems that arise in the classroom and try to work out better ways of doing things.

To foster a sense of worth

Treat children as you treat your own good friends: find kindly, personal things to say; notice and comment on the positive things a child does.

Try to convey to pupils that you like them, that you have faith in them, that when something goes wrong you will try to help and to see their side of the situation.

Be friendly to *all* children and go out of your way to give an extra dose of friendliness to those who need it most—the noisy ones; the slow ones; the shy ones; the ones with problems such as divorce, illness, or unemployment in the family.

See that each child has a chance to taste success in some area—reading, singing, drawing, pantomiming, playing, caring for a classroom pet, or cleaning the chalkboard.

Build on a child's strengths, then help the child master his or her difficulties.

Keep in mind that praise for what a child has done, or tried hard to do, is a tonic that inspires greater efforts.

Evaluate a child's own progress rather than comparing him or her with others.

Help children learn to accept mistakes and to profit from them. But try to see that pupils have a variety of opportunities for successful experiences too.

Assume that a child having difficulty *wants* to learn but for some reason or other is not doing so; then try to seek the causes for the difficulty. Make use of personnel on the school staff—counselors, nurse, speech therapists, learning-disability specialists, psychologists, and so on—in seeking solutions.

Plan classroom activities to fit the abilities of each child in your room. Set goals for a child that are possible for him or her to achieve. Do not ask a child to achieve what is impossible.

Remember that the child's achievement can often be facilitated if you, the teacher, utilize all the helps at hand—supervisory bulletins, teacher's guides and resource books, courses of study, multimedia aids, an individualized curriculum, as well as sound, appealing instructional aids for pupils.

Signs and Symptoms of Illness[1]

Point of Observation	Physical Signs	Behavior	Complaint
General Appearance and Behavior	Excessive thinness or excessive overweight; very small or very large in body build for age; pallor; weary expression; fatigue; poor posture; dark circles or puffiness under eyes.	Acts tired or apathetic; is easily irritated; makes frequent trips to toilet; has persistent nervous habits, such as muscular twitching or biting of nails or lips; is subject to spasms (fits), fainting spells, or frequent nosebleeds; gets short of breath after mild exertion and climbing stairs; lacks appetite; vomits frequently.	Feels tired or is apathetic; doesn't want to play; has aches or pains; feels sick to stomach; feels dizzy.
Ears	Discharge from ear; cotton in ear; tired, strained expression long before day is over; watchful, bewildered expression.	Is persistently inattentive; asks to have questions repeated; habitually fails to respond when questioned; mispronounces common words; cocks one ear toward speaker.	Has earache; has buzzing or ringing in ears; ears feel stuffy; hears noises in head; feels dizzy.
Eyes	Inflamed (reddened) or watery eyes; frequent sties; crusted lids; cross-eye.	Holds book too close to eyes; squints at book or chalkboard; persistently rubs or blinks eyes; reads poorly.	Headache; eyes ache or smart; cannot see well (blurred vision).
Nose and Throat (Upper Respiratory Tract)	Frequent or long-continued colds; persistent nasal discharge.	Is frequently absent from school because of a cold; constantly clears throat or has frequent coughing or sneezing spells; is always sniffling or blowing nose; breathes persistently through mouth.	Throat feels sore or scratchy; has difficulty in swallowing; nose feels stuffy or sore.
Skin	Rashes or inflamed skin areas; scales and crusts; persistent sores; pimples and blackheads on face; boils; hives; persistent warts; accidental injuries, such as cuts.	Is always scratching himself; is subject to skin irritations (hives, eczema, puzzling rashes, etc.) which suggest sensitivity to one or more substances (allergic manifestations); is easily bruised.	Skin itches or burns.

[1] Courtesy of the Metropolitan Life Insurance Company.

A Developmental Profile of Nine- to Ten-Year-Olds

Health education, if it is to be effective, must be appropriate to the developmental level of the learner. The combined knowledge and talents of the author-consultant-advisor team (see pages T4 and T5) brought together to aid in creating this Program have yielded a highly useful profile of nine- to ten-year-olds. This profile was used as background for developing the pupil's textbook and related materials. While it is true that there is no typical child, certain characteristics which seem to be predominant in this age group are described below.

Many concerns related to mental health are present

Nine- to ten-year-olds want to understand themselves. They welcome the chance to stop and think about themselves—their strengths, weaknesses, and special interests.

Children this age are relieved to find out that others, like themselves, experience feelings of frustration, fear, anger, and shyness. It reassures these youngsters to learn some helpful ways of dealing with strong feelings.

Conforming is important

Nine- to ten-year-olds are generally conformists, suspicious of anything that is different. They need help in accepting those who are not just like themselves.

Interest in clubs and close groups of friends is stronger now than in previous years. However, the membership and purpose of these groups changes frequently. And members are almost always of the same sex.

The influence of the group is becoming more pronounced. Children want to be like the others, to talk and dress like them.

The attention span has increased

Boys and girls of this age have ideas and interests of their own and are capable of carrying them out. They may spend an entire morning or afternoon at home with an Erector set or chemistry outfit or with projects and hobbies of various kinds. However, as soon as a project no longer interests these youngsters, they may drop it without finishing it or giving it further thought.

Perfectionism is evident

Nine- to ten-year-olds may work hard to perfect a skill and to do things the right way. They are no longer satisfied just to draw or paint a picture; they are more critical of their product and may ask help with perspective. Technique becomes of greater importance, though too much adult emphasis can destroy interest.

Play skills are important

Nines and Tens want to know how to pitch, catch, and bat a ball well. Both boys and girls are eager to learn how to do such things as swim, folk dance, roller-skate, or ice-skate.

Because of the pronounced interest in acquiring play skills, this is a good year for parents and teachers to encourage youngsters to learn how to do things and to help them do these things with increasing skill.

Active, rough-and-tumble play is enjoyed

Many children this age enjoy active, vigorous play activities. Shouting and tearing around and "rough stuff" are not uncommon. However, at times nine- to ten-year-olds may also meet in groups to just sit around and talk.

Efforts to develop standards are apparent

Fairness plays a large part in the thinking of nine- and ten-year-olds. There are many arguments over fairness in games. This sign indicates that these children are developing standards of right and wrong.

Physically, most nine- to ten-year-olds are very much like eight-year-olds

They are, however, a little longer legged, a little better developed, and a little closer to maturity. Most youngsters may make little gain in height or weight during this period. A few may begin to experience the rapid growth spurt of the preadolescent period. Some girls are growing faster than boys and may be one to two years ahead of boys their age. A very few girls may begin to menstruate during this year.

The lungs and the digestive and circulatory systems are still growing and are almost mature in function.

The hands are becoming increasingly skillful. Some children are beginning to show much greater skill than others.

Permanent teeth continue to come in

First and second bicuspids are appearing and problems in tooth alignment are becoming evident. If correction seems to be indicated, the dentist should be consulted. Treatment is sometimes started at this age level, since the growth of mouth and facial tissue during this period facilitates realignment of the teeth.

While teeth are no longer a subject of top interest, nine- to ten-year-olds still have many questions about the teeth. They want to know about the structure and care of the teeth, the work of the dentist, ways to avoid cavities, and reasons why some children need braces and others don't.

Health concerns are many

Nine- to ten-year-olds are very curious about the body, its structure and functioning. However, studies show that this age group asks more questions about *germs and diseases* than about any other topic. Other often asked questions are:

"What would happen if you had no brain?"
"What happens if you don't eat the right foods?"
"How much sleep do I really need?"
"If you don't get enough exercise, what will happen to you?"
"What do you do for a burn?"
"What illnesses do you get from smoking?"
"Am I growing the way I should?"

Interests are expanding to community health

This age group shows lively interest in air pollution, water pollution, noise pollution, litter, and ways to dispose of solid wastes. They are now capable of using many reference books that are available in order to extend their interests.

Safety can be a problem

Chief among the accidents that occur in this age group are water accidents, bicycle accidents, and falls. Pedestrian accidents are also common. A surprising number of nine- to ten-year-olds need to learn where to walk on a road if there are no sidewalks.

This is a good time, too, to consider safety with drugs; with special emphasis on not experimenting with strange pills or other drugs, including alcohol.

The Parent—Teacher Conference

A conference, for our purposes, means a face-to-face conversation between a teacher and a parent. The conference may be a part of the regularly scheduled school program or it may be called by the teacher to discuss a problem. Sometimes the parent initiates the conference because of a special concern.

Whether the goal is to become acquainted with parents, to report on how things are going in school subjects, or to work out a health problem or some other difficulty, teachers as well as parents can learn and profit from such an exchange of ideas.

A conference may last fifteen minutes or fifty. The teacher may have one or several conferences with a child's parents in the course of a school year. In any case, the pooling of information can result in a better understanding of the child and of ways in which the parents and the teacher can work together to help the youngster.

A conference calls for careful preparation. You will want to organize your thoughts in advance to be clear about what you wish to accomplish. And you may want to gather records and samples of the pupil's written work to go over with parents.

You may also want to collect information from the school nurse, the counselor, the speech therapist, and so on to have available as you explain referrals for medical or other attention.

Much that a teacher takes for granted about how children grow in the ability to share, to compromise, to take responsibility, to be self-reliant, and to be considerate of others is news to parents. You may need to explain that all children have basic emotional needs but that these needs show up in entirely different ways in different children.

What Do Parents Want to Know?

Parents want to know what and how their children are being taught. A comment such as "George is doing well" doesn't mean much to parents. More helpful is an explanation such as "George likes health. He uses some of his free time to read books about health. He reports on the books to the class, and that shows he's getting the sense of what he is reading."

Many parents want to know if there is anything they can do at home to help their child with schoolwork. You can suggest word games and number games to play at home that will augment skills without putting parents in the role of tutors.

Parents want, and should be able to get, an accurate interpretation of group-testing results given in laymen's terms. One cannot take for granted that parents know the nature of tests used.

In addition to information on academic achievement, parents often need and appreciate help on special health problems of their youngsters. Along with the school nurse, the teacher can help parents locate the community resources available for vision, speech, and hearing difficulties; dental care; immunizations; chest X rays; and emergency attention.

Ending the Conference

Close the conference on an optimistic note in order to send parents on the way with a good feeling about the conference and about their child. A minute's summary and a word about a future meeting is often useful. If that is not a sufficient signal that good-bys are in order, you can always stand up, mention that someone is waiting, and thank the parents for coming.

The "How" of Health Teaching

Effective health teaching uses a variety of learning experiences. Some techniques that have been found helpful are suggested below.

Talking Things Over

Group discussion is a valuable technique. It *does* pay to talk things over. In fact, there is research to indicate that a change in attitude can be effected as a result of *talking things over in a group discussion*. In guiding group discussion:

Give students a chance to think before they talk.

Refer questions back to students now and then; for example, "Helen, why do you think that?" or "Jim, do you agree?"

Don't call on the first child who volunteers. Wait and see if you can bring into the discussion a child who rarely volunteers.

Listen to a student's remarks and make some supporting comment about them.

Once in a while inject an informal note by telling of your own experiences.

Don't hesitate to bring up important ideas students do not think of. If possible, ask questions to bring out these ideas.

Tactfully divert the discussion from private or family information.

Use open-ended stories to foster discussion.

Summarize the main points of the discussion and encourage the group to try out the ideas gained from the discussion.

Taking Trips

Children can gain much from such experiences as visiting a water-treatment plant to see how water is purified. Preparation for field trips should include talking over what is to be seen, what questions may be answered, and what behavior is appropriate. Follow-up activities should include a chance for sharing information.

Seeing Films and Filmstrips

Films and filmstrips are always a special treat and can be effective aids. A carefully selected list is provided on pages T39–T45.

It is advisable to preview materials before the actual showing. This will enable you to call attention to important points or to raise questions that will be answered in the film. After the showing, give children an opportunity to discuss ideas they have gained.

Dramatizing and Pantomiming

Youngsters love dramatizing, pantomiming, and role playing. These activities can be used profitably at times in connection with health and safety concepts.

Enjoying Poetry

Many an important lesson is imparted joyously through a poem. What is more, children often ask to hear a favorite poem over and over. In this way the message is reinforced by repetition. Throughout the texts in this Program, good use is made of appropriate poems by well-known writers for children.

Enjoying Books

The school and public libraries are wonderful sources of good children's books that convey health information in charming ways and that can be read to or by youngsters.

There are also books "to grow on," or books that deal in helpful ways with such problems as feeling left out, making friends, and learning to cope with difficulties. See pages T39–T45 for suggested books.

Movement Exploration and Games

Children grow in physical well-being as they participate in vigorous muscular activity, although there are individual differences in the amount of activity required. All the body systems benefit, and endurance is improved as a result of a continuous program of guided exercise.

Youngsters grow in self-confidence and emotional maturity as they improve in fitness, gain skills, and apply the skills to such activities as games, sports, stunts, and dance. Moreover, they learn to understand and accept their own capabilities, strengths, and weaknesses, as well as those of other children.

Movement Exploration in Physical Education

Perhaps your pupils have had experience in movement exploration in preceding years. Even so, you will want to allow some time for further exploration. Remember, though, that while young children find joy merely in experimenting with different movements, middle-graders like to know *why* they are experimenting. Thus they might experiment with *changing direction*, as they will need to do in playing basketball. Or they might experiment with *dodging movements*, such as they make use of in class games.

Many variations and combinations are possible when children are exploring basic movements such as skipping, sliding, or galloping; changing the direction of the movement; changing the speed from fast to slow. The following characteristics might be explored:[1]

1. Size of movement (large, small)
2. Speed of movement (fast, slow)
3. Direction of movement (forward, backward, sideward)
4. Level of movement (high, medium, low)
5. Force of movement (strong, weak, heavy, light)
6. Path of movement (straight, curving, spiraling, zigzagging)
7. Design or shape of movement (changing position of the parts of the body; for example, legs, arms, head).

In their booklet *A Guide to Movement Exploration*,[2] Hackett and Jenson comment: ". . . By experiencing multitudinous movement patterns and physical changes, the child . . . realizes that he is neither best nor worst in every activity; rather these extreme positions are shared by everyone at one time or another."

If you want to investigate more fully the many valuable activities that can be carried out in movement exploration, you will find suggested references on page T20.

Some Favorite Games

The following games have interest and challenge for nine- and ten-year-olds. Movement exploration problems utilizing the skills of a particular game can be presented before that game is played.

Free Ball Tag
Skills to be explored: Running through space, twisting and turning, throwing a ball, changing direction, throwing at a moving target, jumping
Equipment: A large bag of balls and a supply of colored arm bands or ties

[1] From page 8, *Exploration of Basic Movements in Physical Education*, copyright 1960 by the Detroit Board of Education. Used by permission.

[2] From *A Guide to Movement Exploration* by Hackett and Jenson, Rev. 1973. Reprinted by permission of Peek Publications, Palo Alto, Ca.

Players: 12 to 16, or total class
Place: Playground, playroom, gymnasium

The children run freely through the play space trying to keep away from the one who is *It*. If *It* hits someone *below the waist* with the ball, that person gets a ball and a colored arm band and becomes *It* as well. Each time someone is hit, he or she becomes *It*, until eventually everyone is caught. This game takes only a short time to play.

Anyone who hits a dodger *above the waist* must sit out the rest of the game.

Tag in Twos
Skills to be explored: Dodging, running, backward, turning and twisting, stopping and starting, tagging safely.
Equipment: Colored arm bands
Players: Any number of groups of two
Place: Playground, playroom, gymnasium

Children choose partners and sit down about two meters from each other. Then one of each pair is designated as a tagger and stands up. On a signal, the ones sitting down get up and each one tries to keep away from his or her partner, the tagger. If tagged, a child becomes a new tagger and his or her partner sits down.

All continue to play *Tag in Twos* until the signal to stop is given.

Accumulative Tag
Skills to be explored: Running, dodging, stopping and starting, turning and twisting, changing level
Equipment: Colored arm bands if desired
Players: 14 or 16, or total group
Place: Playground, playroom, gymnasium

In the play space allotted, one person is chosen to be *It*. *It* tags someone and that

person is also *It*. Now there are two. They both chase the other players and if they catch two, then there are *four* people who are *It*. They continue until only one or two are left untagged.

The teacher has to be on the alert in this game. Because the game is over quickly, it is important that the teacher stop the action when just one or two are left untagged.

How can the children tell who is *It?* (Colored ties should be placed out of bounds on one side of the play space. When a person has been tagged, the new *It* must get a tie or band and put it on his or her arm or wrist before tagging the other players.)

Animal Hunt
Skills to be explored: Dodging, running through space, jumping, throwing a ball, throwing at a moving target
Equipment: Several 15-cm rubber balls
Players: Total class or small groups
Place: Playground, playroom, gymnasium

Three or four players are chosen as *Hunters* and are each given a 15-cm rubber ball. At the signal, the hunt begins. The other players, the *Animals*, roam freely around the play space and try to keep away from the *Hunters*. If an *Animal* is hit with a ball, the animal must collapse where he or she is and remain at that spot until the game is over. If children have a collision, they too must collapse at the spot where the collision occurred.

The game is completed when a time span is completed—"How many *Animals* can the *Hunters* get in two minutes?"—or when all the *Animals* have been caught. New *Hunters* are chosen from those who have not been caught.

Punch Ball

Skills to be explored: Running through space, making punching actions, running with a ball, dodging, changing directions

Equipment: Fifteen to twenty 20-cm rubber balls

Players: As many as there are 20-cm balls available for use—or small groups

Place: Playground, playroom, gymnasium

Each player carries a 20-cm ball under one arm. On the signal, each person tries to punch the ball from someone else's arm. If a person loses a ball, the person must retrieve it and sit down on the floor. The winners can be those who still remain in the game after one minute, or the winner can be the last person to remain in the game with a ball under one arm.

If children have collisions, punch a player instead of the ball, or are chased out of bounds, they are out of the game and must sit on the floor.

Physical Education References

Anderson, Marian H., et al. *Play with a Purpose: Elementary School Physical Education.* 2d ed. Harper, 1972.

Association for Childhood Education International. *Physical Education for Children's Healthful Living.* ACEI, 1968.

Barlin, Anne, and Barlin, Paul. *The Art of Learning Through Movement.* Ward Ritchie, 1971.

Carr, Rachel E. *Be a Frog, a Bird, or a Tree: Creative Yoga Exercises for Children.* Doubleday, 1973.

Dauer, Victor P. *Dynamic Physical Education for Elementary School Children.* 5th ed. Burgess, 1975.

Diamondstein, Geraldine. *Children Dance in the Classroom.* Macmillan, 1971.

Fabricius, Helen. *Physical Education for the Classroom Teacher.* 2d ed. W. C. Brown, 1972.

Films and Filmstrips for the Teacher

Series of twenty-four cartridged film-loops: *Basic Movement* (6 loops); *Movement Awareness* (5 loops); *Basic Manipulative Activities* (7 loops); *Functional Fitness* (6 loops) (Ealing Films).

Introduction to Body Movements: Locomotor Skills (Silver Burdett).

Learning Through Movement (S-L Productions).

Series of four films: *Movement Education: Guided Exploration;* *Movement Education in Physical Education; Movement Education: The Problem-Solving Technique; Movement Education: Time and Space Awareness* (University of Iowa).

A Time to Move (Early Childhood Productions).

Family-Life Education

Ideally sex education should be given at home from the time the child asks questions about how babies are born. The part that the home plays in teaching a child about life and how it begins is indeed important.

The Scott, Foresman HEALTH Program offers a variety of aids to schools and to parents. In the pupils' textbooks of this Program at all levels, strong and persistent efforts are made to foster communication between each child and his or her family. At the end of each chapter, there is a section entitled "School and Home." Here boys and girls are encouraged to talk over with the family the health and safety ideas they are learning at school; to share in the work of the family; to seek additional information from family members; and to talk over their problems, questions, or feelings. With communications channels kept open, children may feel more free to ask questions about birth and reproduction too.

Also in this Program, much emphasis is put on developing warm human relationships. Thus from the outset children are led to think about what we mean by love—caring and sharing—and about ways of showing our love. In the same way, youngsters later explore kindness and ways of showing it. Boys and girls in the intermediate grades are encouraged to reach out to others, to share something of themselves with others, and to offer help and comfort when it is needed.

The idea that all human beings have feelings such as those of love, joy, shyness, fear, and anger is emphasized. And ways of dealing with strong feelings are considered. Such very human approaches and emphases offer a background against which more specific sex-education instruction can be given.

Supplementary Material

A supplementary booklet entitled *The Human Story: Facts on Birth, Growth, and Reproduction* is available for schools that wish to use it with their own family-living courses. This booklet, designed for pupils aged ten to fourteen, was written by Sadie Hofstein, with Julius B. Richmond, M.D., as special consultant.

The booklet answers many of the questions that students in this age group ask about their growing bodies, about reproduction and how babies are born, and about the way heredity affects their lives. It is suitable for classroom use and might also be sent home for pupils to share with parents.

Cooperation with Parents

Some parents who feel inadequate to give their children needed information will turn to the school and to the teacher for help and advice. The well-informed teacher can do much to cooperate with parents, both through individual conferences and through well-planned open-house or PTA programs.

Because many parents find it difficult to talk to their children about sexuality or to answer questions in this area, they appreciate knowing about books or booklets that can be of help. Some books and booklets that can be recommended are listed on page T22.

Explaining Menstruation

It is possible that a girl may begin her first menstrual period at school. Even if she has been well prepared for the onset of menstruation by her parents, this first occasion may evoke anxiety. Then, too, it is quite possible that some girls may not have been prepared by explanations at home. The range of age for the onset of menstration is great—from nine years on, although twelve to thirteen is perhaps average. Because some parents do not realize the immediacy of their preadolescent daughter's need for information, many girls are not prepared adequately for the experience.

In the event that the onset of the first menstruation does occur at school, the school nurse might be called upon to provide a sanitary pad and to offer reassurance and explanation. In some instances, however, *you*, the teacher may have to explain in a simple way such facts as these:

Physical maturity for a girl means that her reproductive organs (ovaries) have developed the power to mature or ripen the ova, or egg cells. An egg leaves one of the ovaries each month and travels down one of the Fallopian tubes to the uterus. The uterus is a pear-shaped organ especially designed to serve as a sort of nest where a new baby can grow if the egg is fertilized.

As soon as the egg leaves the ovary, the blood supply to the uterus is increased so that, in case the egg should be fertilized, there would be nourishment for the developing baby. When the egg is not fertilized, it disintegrates. The extra blood sent to the uterus is not needed, so the blood is discharged through the vagina. This is the menstrual flow. It usually lasts for about three to five days, but it may last for a longer or a shorter time.

Questions should be encouraged and answered in a straightforward manner, without hint of mystery or embarrassment. Menstruation is a healthy aspect of normal development for a girl.

For Children

Gruenberg, Sidonie M., and Gruenberg, Benjamin. *The Wonderful Story of You.* Doubleday, 1960. For third through sixth graders.

NEA-AMA Joint Committee on Health Problems in Education. *A Story About You.* Rev. ed. AMA and NEA, 1975. Designed for youngsters from nine to twelve.

For Parents and Teachers

Anderson, Wayne J. *How to Explain Sex to Children.* Denison, 1971.

Child Study Association of America. *What to Tell Your Children About Sex.* Rev. ed. Pocket Books, 1974.

NEA-AMA Joint Committee on Health Problems in Education. *Facts Aren't Enough.* AMA and NEA, 1973.

————. *Parents' Responsibility.* Rev. ed. AMA and NEA, 1970.

Films for Classroom Use

Boy to Man (Churchill).

Girl to Woman (Churchill).

The Human Body: Reproductive System (Coronet).

Films About Menstruation

Naturally . . . A Girl (Association-Sterling, produced by Personal Products Co.).

The Story of Menstruation (The Life-Cycle Center, Kimberly-Clark Corp., produced by Walt Disney Productions).

If Children Ask About Death[1]

By Gladys Gardner Jenkins

Children are curious about the beginnings of life. They are also curious about death. As teachers, we may be called upon to answer children's questions about death, to comfort a bereaved child, or on rare occasion to tell of the death of a classmate. At such times, we need to remember that the child's capacity to understand death will depend upon cognitive development plus experience.

One factor involved in understanding death is the cognitive knowledge of the facts of death as the end of life in the body. These facts can be given by a sensitive teacher as a child comes upon death—the flowers that die, the dead bird found on a walk, the death of a classroom gerbil. Later, as children gradually come to understand and appreciate the life cycle as it affects all living things, death will be put in perspective.

But understanding death also involves deep feelings. By the careful choice of stories children can be drawn into some of the feelings and concerns we all have about the death of a person for whom we care. Children have responded for many years to E. B. White's book *Charlotte's Web* (Harper).

However, some books today are presented with such realism that they may precipitate anxiety in children instead of developing understanding. For instance, a realistic presentation of the death of a grandparent may arouse anxiety in a child who had never thought of the death of a loved grandparent as imminent. A picture of the end of all living things might be a forceful lesson in ecology but a devastating thought for a young child.

[1] This article has been added to the *Teacher's Supplement* at the request of many teachers who have used previously published health materials by Scott, Foresman and Company.

Learning to accept reality is important. But the readiness of a child to be faced with reality which does not come from experience must be carefully weighed. It may be harmful rather than useful to stimulate imagination and provoke thoughts before the child has the resources to cope with them.

It is difficult to know what children are actually feeling, what their concerns, interpretations, and thoughts about death may be. This is why it is important to provide an atmosphere in the classroom in which children will feel free to ask questions and share ideas if the subject of death occurs.

Teachers may also be called upon to help children in their classrooms when the experience of death touches them through the loss of a parent, grandparent, sibling, friend, or classmate. This occasion may also call for facts, but the facts will now be interspersed with deep emotional feelings.

Death of one who has been close becomes a painful separation. Some children feel angry: "Why did my father leave me?" Many children, and many adults, have a feeling of guilt: "What did I do?" This feeling can be very strong and add anxiety to the grief of separation. A child should be reassured by being told the real cause of the death. There is also a fear that others whom the child loves may die, leaving the child with no one to care for him or her. Again, reassurance is needed.

Many children cannot express these feelings in words but show them in behavior. A child may become more demanding of attention or may cling to an adult. Older children may be so full of their thoughts that they can no longer focus on their schoolwork. Some children may not want to play with

T23

their friends or take part in activities which they previously had enjoyed. Others cover their feelings by being aggressive or by acting as if nothing had happened. These are clues that the children need our help.

Grief in a child must have an outlet. The child who seems so brave, who does not cry, who goes about life as usual may be bottling up a deep grief that may cause difficulty at a later time. It does not help children to tell them to be brave, not to cry, to be a big boy or girl. Children need to grieve for a time. Neither does it help for adults to hide their grief, although hysterical grief can be deeply disturbing to children.

It is not wise to arouse thoughts of extra responsibilities such as: "You will be the man of the house" or "You will be the little mother now." Neither is it helpful to use the memory of the person who has died to encourage effort or better behavior. These are burdens a child is not able to carry. Such suggestions only build anxiety. In addition, it is better to talk about memories of a real person rather than a glorified one.

The most helpful support we can give as teachers is to let the child know that we do understand the mixed-up feelings, that we are ready to listen if talk would help, and that we will answer questions as honestly as we can. Often, too, the physical comfort of an arm around the child, or a shoulder on which to cry, can bring great relief.

If a child in the class dies, the other children will be tense and anxious. They can more easily accept death for old people than for another child whom they have known. The death of a classmate may arouse fear of death for oneself. The children should be told the truth about their classmate's death. It is wise to help them talk about it and to help them share their feelings and concerns. Discuss what they would like to remember about their classmate and what could be done as a special remembrance.

Such an open discussion may lead to questions about death. Some children may want to talk about the funeral, about burial, or about cremation. It can be explained that different groups of people have different customs or their own special ways of saying good-by. The most difficult questions to answer will be those that might be raised about life after death. The children will come from homes of many religious faiths. What they have been taught at home will influence what they believe to be true. Each religious faith explains what happens according to its own beliefs. A teacher should neither contradict the religious teaching of the home nor express his or her own religious beliefs.

Here are some books that can help a teacher meet situations involving death.

Grollman, Earl A. *Explaining Death to Children.* Beacon Press, 1967.

Harris, Audrey. *Why Did He Die?* Lerner, 1971.

Jackson, Edgar N. *Telling a Child About Death.* Hawthorn Books, 1965.

Kübler-Ross, Elisabeth. *Questions and Answers on Death and Dying.* Macmillan, 1974.

Mitchell, Marjorie Editha. *The Child's Attitude to Death.* Schocken, 1967.

Stein, Sara Bonnett. *About Dying.* Walker, 1974.

Enrichment Suggestions for Chapter 1
Getting to Know Yourself and Others[1]

Overview

Chapter One, which focuses on mental health, including personal and social growth, promotes each child's self-image and feelings of worth. Students discover ways in which they are like others and ways in which they are different from others. They consider what makes a person likeable and learn ways to deal with strong feelings such as those of anger, fear, and shyness. Students also consider the problem of whether or not to do what others are doing. And they read a non-threatening, gentle treatment of how to comfort a friend whose pet has died.

Important Ideas Developed in the Chapter

No person is exactly the same as any other.

Everyone likes to be noticed, to be known by name, to be liked, and to have friends.

People in a group can get better acquainted when they share some information about themselves.

Each person is like others in many ways.

Willingness to share, to take turns, to keep promises, to treat others kindly, and to help others are qualities of likeable people.

Everyone feels shy or scared at times.

When you feel shy or scared, it helps to talk over your feelings.

Often it helps to go ahead and do the thing you are scared of doing; the scared feelings may soon go away.

Everyone has angry feelings at times.

Try talking things over when you are angry instead of hitting or hurting others.

Physical activity, or some other pleasurable activity can help work off angry feelings until they can be talked out.

At times everyone has hard decisions to make; learning to make wise decisions on your own is a part of growing up.

It helps, in grieving for a dead pet, to talk things out with others; crying can help too.

When a pet dies, you can remember it and keep a part of it alive in your memory.

Behavioral Objectives

See page 32 in the pupil's book where behavioral objectives in the cognitive area are posed directly to pupils in simple terms.

See also some hoped-for objectives, mainly in the affective area, set forth in the "Teacher's Notes" for page 32.

8-9 *Getting to Know Yourself and Others* (Chapter-Opening Pages)

You might set aside space on the bulletin board for students to post self-portraits or photographs of themselves. Such a human-interest bulletin board can set the stage for this chapter.

10 *Preview It*

Students may want to start answering some of the questions posed by various titles in the chapter. If so, do not allot much time for this activity. This section is intended to arouse interest and curiosity and to open the students' minds to what they are to learn.

11-13 *What Is Special About You?*

Students might write a paragraph on "What Is Special About Me." Volunteers could read aloud their paragraphs or post them on a special display board.

---

[1] See page T39 for Reference Materials related to this chapter.

14 *How Are You Like Others?*

You might poll the class to find how many have dogs, cats, gerbils, or other pets.

15-16 *What Makes People Likeable?*

Pupils could role-play things a likeable person might do with a new yoyo: share it, show someone how to use it, tell what store it came from. Others could role-play what a not-so-likeable person might do: refuse to share it, brag about how well he or she can use it, put down someone who tries it.

17-18 *What Can You Do About Scared Feelings?*

Volunteers might role-play different ways to deal with scared feelings about doing a new page of math problems.

19-20 *What Can You Do About Angry Feelings?*

Another way to work off angry feelings is to write about them. If you think a friend has treated you unfairly, you might write an angry letter, telling how you feel and why. Writing the letter often helps dispel the angry feelings—and you can then throw away the letter. When you feel calmer about the situation, you can talk over the matter with the friend. You may even find there was a misunderstanding between you.

21 *Enjoy It*

Pupils might enjoy drawing themselves looking like lemons or apples.

22-24 *Do You Have to Do What Others Are Doing?*

Volunteers might role-play various ways of dealing with such situations as these:

A friend offers you a sip out of a can of beer.
Someone asks to copy your math paper.
Some children you know suggest you sneak off and try smoking a cigarette.
Allow plenty of time for discussion of the suggested solutions.

25-26 *What Can Help When a Pet Dies?*

You might try to obtain at the library the January-February 1975 issue of the magazine *Children Today*. Read the excellent article "Why Isn't the Gerbil Moving Anymore?" (Discussing Death in the Classroom—and at Home) by Gerald P. Koocher.

27 *Write It*

Allot time for volunteers to read aloud what they have written. Students' writings might also be put in a class scrapbook along with drawings depicting feelings.

28-29 *Feelings*

You might display the students' unsigned drawings on a bulletin board under the feelings each drawing expresses, or put them into the class scrapbook.

30 *Health Around Us*

Give pupils a few days to look around for things that give them happy feelings. (A pretty flower box, grass growing from cracks in a walk.) Provide time for students to report on what they have seen.

31 *Things to Do*

Students might unscramble the following words: *grany, yellon, phyap, soulaje.*

32-35 *Reviews, Tests, School and Home*

Enrichment Suggestions for Chapter 2
Discovering Some Wonders of the Human Body[1]

Overview

Chapter Two focuses on what has been called "that miracle, the human body." Deep respect for the body is engendered as students learn some of the intricacies of the body's structure and functioning. The material includes descriptions of the body's reserve power and its many protective devices.

Important Ideas Developed in the Chapter

The skin can stretch and fold; it grows as a person grows.

The fingerprints of each human being are unique.

Pigment in the skin gives the skin its color. Except for differing amounts of pigment, the skin of every human being is the same.

The skin helps regulate body temperature.

Human beings are warm-blooded.

The heart pumps blood through blood vessels to all parts of the body.

The heartbeat speeds up during strenuous exercise and during emotional stress; it slows down during sleep.

The pacemaker in the heart sets the pace for the heartbeat.

The body stores food and water for use in emergencies.

The body has immense reserve power and it has many automatic protective actions.

The body has five main senses as well as the senses of hunger and thirst, the muscle sense, the sense of direction, and the sense of balance.

Messages from all parts of the body are sent to the brain over *sensory nerves;* messages go from the brain to the muscles over *motor nerves.*

[1] See page T40 for Reference Materials related to this chapter.

Behavioral Objectives

See page 66 in the pupil's book where behavioral objectives in the cognitive area are posed directly to pupils.

See also some hoped-for objectives, mainly in the affective area, set forth in the "Teacher's Notes" for page 66.

36–37 *Discovering Some Wonders of the Human Body* (Chapter-Opening Pages)

The questions on these pages help set the stage for learning. Students turn their attention to what it is they are going to study. They are also encouraged to think of special things in the area that they want to find out.

38 *Preview It*

Students may want to try answering some of the questions posed by the various titles in the chapter. Do not allot much time for this activity. This section is designed to arouse interest and curiosity, and to open pupils' minds to what they are to learn.

39–41 *What Is Wonderful About Your Skin?*

Another interesting fact is that perspiration, especially "sweaty palms," often accompanies strong emotions.

42–45 *What Is Remarkable About Your Heart?*

You might explain that the heart is really *two* pumps. These two pumps are side by side and they work at the same time, but they are separated by a wall of muscle. The pump on the right side of the heart pumps blood to the lungs. The pump on the left side of the heart pumps blood to all parts of the body.

The artificial pacemaker is just one of many advances in medical science. See if pupils know of other advances; for example, an artificial voice box that can be implanted to do the work of a real one that has to be removed. Artificial joints, such as hip joints or finger joints, can be used to replace real ones. And artificial blood vessels can be used to replace portions of real ones.

46 *How Does Your Body Store Food and Water?*

Point out, if pupils do not, that solid waste leaves the body in what is called a *bowel movement.* Waste water is called *urine.*

47 *What Reserve Power Does Your Body Have?*

New ways are being invented to help the blind to "see." One machine is the Optacon reading machine. The blind person moves a tiny camera over a page with one hand while the other hand is in a feeler box. The camera sends raised pictures of letters to the feeler box. The blind person feels the outlines of the letters with a fingertip.

48–49 *What Protective Actions Does Your Body Have?*

The action of the ring of muscles in the esophagus is called *peristalsis.* Because of the action of these muscles that squeeze and push along the food, it would be possible for a person to swallow while standing on his or her head.

50–51 *Enjoy It*

Students might try modeling from clay their own versions of the body in action.

The group might make a scrapbook of poems they find about how senses make life more pleasant. Some students may want to write poems of their own to include in the scrapbook. Remind them that poems do not have to rhyme.

52–53 *How Do Your Senses Help?*

Students might do an experiment at home to find what it would be like to have no sense of smell. They could try eating two or three tasty foods while holding their noses and being blindfolded. Then they could report back to the class about how the food tasted and about whether they could identify the food by taste.

54 *Write It*

Group poems, like the one on this page, are created with ease once pupils have a form that gives the poem unity. The form used here is a repetitive one, "A wonder is . . . ." When pupils are comfortable with a form, they usually have much to say.

55–56 *What Is Wonderful About Your Brain?*

This is a good time to point out that sometimes the wonderful brain doesn't work so well. When it is tired, for example, you can not think as well as you usually do. You may make mistakes or forget things.

57–64 *Some Wonders of the Human Body (Picture Essay)*

65 *Things to Do*

Students might unscramble the following words: *neses, olbod, velir, nobe.*

66–69 *Reviews, Tests, School and Home*

Enrichment Suggestions for Chapter 3
Becoming Safety-Minded[1]

Overview

Chapter Three stresses safety knowledge that is needed to prevent the most serious accidents and those that occur with greatest frequency: motor vehicle accidents, falls, water accidents, burns, and scalds. A picture essay describes dangerous places to play. And safety in using medicines (drugs) is discussed in a positive way.

Important Ideas Developed in the Chapter

When walking on a road with no sidewalk, keep to the left.

When walking at night, wear reflective material or tape, wear something light, or carry a light.

Look both ways and behind you for turning cars before crossing a street; cross only at corners or in crosswalks.

A bicycle driver must know and obey the same traffic-safety rules as a car driver.

To avoid falls when climbing trees, climb only trees with low branches and rough bark; stay off dead branches.

To avoid falls at home, keep objects off stairs, wipe up spilled liquids at once, use handrails, and use ladders to reach objects on high shelves.

Dangerous places for play are quarries, dumps, parking lots, empty buildings, and construction areas.

To help a person in trouble in the water, try to extend something for the person to grab onto; get adult help if possible.

Use survival floating if you should ever be in trouble in the water.

Medicines (drugs) should be used only when needed and exactly according to directions.

[1] See page T41 for Reference Materials related to this chapter.

Behavioral Objectives

See page 94 in the pupil's book where behavioral objectives in the cognitive area are posed directly to pupils.

See also some hoped-for objectives, mainly in the affective area, set forth in the "Teacher's Notes" for page 94.

70–71 *Becoming Safety-Minded* (Chapter-Opening Pages)

Questions on these pages get pupils "in the spirit" of the chapter and make them curious about its contents.

72 *Preview It*

You might write on the chalkboard the main questions raised by titles in this chapter. This will provide an idea of what is to be learned.

73–74 *How Can You Be a Safe Pedestrian?*

Remind students that when they are walking in a group, each person should try to keep as careful as when he or she is walking alone. Sometimes group members just follow along and fail to observe their usual caution.

75–78 *How Can You Be a Safe Bicycle Driver?*

Discuss with pupils this bicycle-safety precaution: To help you be safe, your bike must fit you.

You might also encourage volunteers to investigate local safety rules for bicycles.

79–80 *How Can You Help Prevent Falls?*

Pupils might keep records of accidents that occur on the playground, in the school halls, in the classroom, or in the gymnasium. Discuss ways to prevent such accidents.

81–85 *Dangerous Places to Play*
         (Picture Essay)

Discuss other unsafe places to play: around railroad tracks or railroad property, on farm machines, in excavations, in abandoned mines, in open pits, on wharves or other waterfront places. Consider with pupils the hazards of each place. If possible, tailor the discussion to hazardous places in the students' community.

86 *Write It*

Students might also compose safety riddles and puzzles. For example, here is a riddle: *You need it in the kitchen. You need it around the stove. It can help keep your hand from getting burned. What is it?* (A potholder)

Scrambled-letter puzzles focusing on safety rules are fun too. For example:

Od otn teg oot losec ot a eather.

(Do not get too close to a heater.)

87–89 *How Can You Help Someone in the*
         Water?

Review some safety precautions for swimmers: Swim only where there is a lifeguard, don't go swimming alone, don't do any rough playing like pushing or ducking in the water, stay out of deep water if you can't swim, come out of the water if a storm starts.

Talk over the dangers of calling for "help" as a joke and of running and chasing around on slippery cement at a pool. Students might give dramatic skits to reinforce some of the above precautions.

A good book for students to read is *No Pushing, No Ducking: Safety in the Water* by Barbara Rinkoff (Lothrop).

90 *Safety Around Us*

Here are some additional precautions in the use of drugs: Directions on prescription drugs should be read carefully for storing instructions. Some drugs should be kept cool and dry; others should be refrigerated.

Medicines that are old should not be used. Many drugs become stale, sometimes harmful, or sometimes ineffective over periods of time. At regular times an adult in the family should clear out the medicine cabinet and dispose of both prescription and over-the-counter drugs that have been on hand for over a year. Prescription drugs are dated as an aid in judging their age. Nonprescription drugs should be dated when purchased.

91–92 *What Should You Know About Drugs?*

Two excellent pamphlets you may want to use as reference material and recommend to parents are *We Want You to Know What We Know About Prescription Drugs* (73–3009) and *We Want You to Know What We Know About Medicines Without Prescriptions* (73–3011). These were prepared by the U.S. Department of Health, Education, and Welfare, Food and Drug Administration. They can be obtained from the Superintendent of Documents, U.S. Government Printing Office, Washington, D.C. 20402.

93 *Things to Do*

Review first aid for cuts: wash with soap and water, apply a sterile bandage, press down on the cut to stop bleeding.

94–97 *Reviews, Tests, School and Home*

Enrichment Suggestions for Chapter 4
Staying Healthy[1]

Overview

Chapter Four stresses the importance of sleep, exercise, and nutrition for good health. Students learn about growth patterns. And the health hazards of smoking are touched upon. The chapter is enlivened by exercises, recipes, a painting by a famous artist, and children's writings.

Important Ideas Developed in the Chapter

Foods affect how you feel; when you are hungry you may feel cross, tired, or restless.

You need the right kinds of foods in the right amounts every day.

A daily food guide can help in planning meal menus and snacks with enough of the right kinds of foods.

The body refreshes itself during sleep when the heart and lungs slow down, many of the big muscles relax, and some parts of the brain are less active.

When you have not had enough sleep, you may feel cross and tired; you may make more mistakes than you ordinarily would.

Children from nine- to ten-years-old need about eleven hours of sleep each night; however sleep needs differ somewhat among individuals.

Exercise helps make strong muscles, helps your heart grow stronger, helps you to work or play strenuously for longer periods without feeling out of breath, and stimulates the appetite.

Games and sports provide much of the exercise you need; they are also fun and offer a means of making new friends.

___
[1] See page T42 for Reference Materials related to this chapter.

Cigarette smoking can cause lung cancer, can be a factor in causing emphysema and other problems in the respiratory system, and can lead to problems in the circulatory system.

Nonsmokers may be annoyed by the smoke from nearby smokers.

Great differences in height, weight, and body-build exist among nine- and ten-year-old boys and girls, all of whom may be quite healthy and growing in the way that is right for them.

Behavioral Objectives

See page 124 in the pupil's book where behavioral objectives in the cognitive area are posed directly to pupils.

See also some hoped-for objectives, mainly in the affective area, set forth in the "Teacher's Notes" for page 124.

98–99 *Staying Healthy*
(Chapter-Opening Pages)

The provocative discussion leads on this page will get the chapter off to a good start.

100 *Preview It*

Pupils may want to start answering some of the questions posed by titles in the chapter. If so, cut this activity short. This section is intended to arouse interest and curiosity and to give pupils an idea of what they are about to learn.

101–105 *How Can Foods Help You Stay Healthy?*

Students might make copies of the food guide on pages 104–105 to take home for discussion with the family and perhaps for posting in the kitchen.

106-107 *What Foods Can You Fix?*

See if pupils can unscramble the following words to find the names of some healthful snacks they can fix for themselves.

ruitf ceiuj *rrocats* *ilkm*
crckersa   *tiufr*   *eeches*

(Answers: fruit juice, carrots, milk, crackers, fruit, cheese.)

108-110 *How Can Sleep Help You Stay Healthy?*

Ask pupils: "Have there been times in your life when you needed more sleep than you do now?" (In early babyhood, they slept most of the time; at age two, they needed twelve or more hours.)

111 *How Can Exercise Help You Stay Healthy?*

Discuss the various ways in which we learn how to play unfamiliar games. We may learn about them from teachers, from Scout or playground leaders, from friends, from older brothers or sisters, and from books.

You can find directions for some appropriate games on pages T19 and T20.

112-113 *Exercises and Activities for Fitness*

Explain to the students that individual differences in performing these exercises and activities are to be expected. Students should do them as best they can.

114 *Enjoy It*

Give pupils a chance to make pictures that "move" like this one, using just a few lines to convey the actions. You might make a class exhibit of their attempts.

115 *Health Around Us*

Sometimes a pupil may comment, "But my mom and dad smoke. Will they get sick?"

You might mention that when many adults started to smoke, they did not know that the habit was harmful. Now we do have the information, and many adults are trying to break the habit. This is hard to do because the habit of smoking is an addiction. However, the concern of their children has caused many parents to try to stop smoking.

We also know that pipe smoking and cigar smoking are not as harmful as cigarette smoking, but these are associated with cancer of the lips, tongue, and throat.

116-117 *How Do You and Others Grow in Healthy Ways?*

Personal charts for boys' and girls' growth records can be obtained from the American Medical Association, 535 N. Dearborn Street, Chicago, Illinois 60610.

118-121 *Some Ways That Boys and Girls Grow* (Picture Essay)

Remind pupils that these are general growth patterns and they do not apply to everyone.

122-123 *Things to Do*

Nine- to ten-year-olds love to make magazines or newspapers. These can be duplicated so each youngster has a copy. Or a huge magazine or newspaper, with giant titles, can be set up on the bulletin board. It can be livened up by family photographs of the students doing healthful things.

124-127 *Reviews, Tests, School and Home*

Enrichment Suggestions for Chapter 5
Learning About Teeth[1]

Overview

Chapter Five satisfies many of the curiosities that nine- to ten-year-olds have about the teeth. Students learn about the make-up of the teeth, the advantages of having teeth of different shapes, ways to prevent tooth decay, and reasons why teeth sometimes come in out of position.

Important Ideas Developed in the Chapter

Teeth help us chew food and speak clearly; they also help give the face its proper shape.

Clean, well-cared for teeth add to personal attractiveness.

The *crown* is the part of the tooth you see; under the gums are the *roots* that help hold the teeth in place.

Each tooth is made up of four kinds of materials: *enamel*, *dentin*, *pulp*, and *cementum*. Elasticlike fibers, the *periodontal membrane*, fasten the tooth to the jawbone.

Each kind of tooth has a special job to do, and every tooth is needed in the mouth.

The four kinds of teeth in the permanent set are *incisors*, *cuspids*, *bicuspids*, and *molars*.

The dentist or dental hygienist can remove harmful *tartar*, or *calculus*, when cleaning your teeth.

Flossing and brushing the teeth daily and cutting down on sweet foods and drinks are ways of helping prevent tooth decay.

Calculus is hardened plaque. Bacteria in plaque work on bits of sweet food left on the teeth; this causes acids that break down the enamel. A cavity, if not filled, spreads into the pulp of the tooth and may

[1] See page T43 for Reference Materials related to this chapter.

cause a toothache and may lead to an abscess.

Behavioral Objectives

See page 148 in the pupil's book where behavioral objectives in the cognitive area are posed directly to pupils.

See also some hoped-for objectives, mainly in the affective area, set forth in the "Teacher's Notes" for page 148.

128–129 *Learning About Teeth*
(Chapter-Opening Pages)

Use the brief overview on this page to stimulate some preliminary discussion. The questions will arouse interest as well as some disagreement. And students will be involved in the subject of teeth and their care.

130 *Preview It*

By the time the average child starts school, he or she has at least three decayed teeth. By age 20, the average young adult has 14 decayed, missing, or filled teeth. Education for preventing tooth decay (and gum disease) is certainly needed.

131 *Why Do You Need Your Teeth?*

You might ask, "Why do you think five-, six-, and seven-year-old children often have some trouble in talking distinctly?" (They are losing primary teeth; without certain teeth, it is difficult to speak clearly.)

132–133 *What Are Teeth Made Of?*

If possible, borrow a model set of teeth from a dentist. Pupils are fascinated by such models and are always surprised by the length and size of the roots of the teeth.

134–136 *Why Are Different-Shaped Teeth Useful?*

If any students have kept their own teeth that have been shed, encourage them to display their collections.

This is a good time to show the film *Dental Health: How and Why* (Coronet). See other film suggestions on page T43.

137–139 *How Can You Take Good Care of Your Teeth?*

A *Plaque Control Kit* (M10) with materials for a class of 35 can be obtained from the American Dental Association, 211 E. Chicago Avenue, Chicago, Illinois 60611. The kit includes soft bristle toothbrushes, dental floss, and disclosing tablets.

The flossing process might also be demonstrated by you, by the school nurse, or by a child who has had special instruction from a dentist or dental hygienist. If floss is available, *all* children might practice flossing.

140–143 *Tooth Decay* and *A Visit to the Dentist* (Picture Essay)

Many questions about the teeth are answered in this picture series. Later, students might make up a play about a child who goes to the dentist to have a cavity filled. The play can show the kinds of conversation that might occur during a visit to the dentist.

144 *Enjoy It*

Students might be interested to know that hundreds of years ago there were barber-surgeons. These barber-surgeons pulled teeth, cut hair, and performed operations. Sometimes, when there weren't any barbers around, blacksmiths pulled teeth. Generally, though, the blacksmiths worked at making things of iron.

Long ago artificial teeth were made of such things as bone, ivory, or wood. About two thousand years ago it was not uncommon to find people fitted with false teeth that were animal teeth—wired to fit in human mouths!

Even in the 1700's, in the early days of our country, dentists did not know how to make well-fitting false teeth. President George Washington had to press his lips against his wooden teeth to help hold his dentures in place.

145 *Health Around Us*

Students might be interested to know of other dental specialists: *pedodontists* who work only with children, *dental research workers* who are trying to find ever-better ways of caring for teeth, and *oral surgeons* who repair broken teeth and extract teeth that are especially hard to remove. *Periodontists* treat diseases of the gum. And *endodontists* work with roots of teeth.

146 *Write It*

A class scrapbook containing students' writings might be made. Information and reports might be added from time to time.

147 *Things to Do*

Volunteers might present a program on proper care of the teeth to the kindergarten and first-grade classes. The program could include posters, skits, and demonstrations of flossing and brushing techniques.

148–151 *Reviews, Tests, School and Home*

Enrichment Suggestions for Chapter 6
Finding Out About Diseases[1]

Overview

In Chapter Six, students learn that communicable diseases are always caused by the harmful kind of germs known as disease germs. Students find out how communicable disease can be spread and what defenses the body has against germs. And they learn how vaccines provide protection against some diseases.

Important Ideas Developed in the Chapter

Communicable diseases are passed from one person to another and are caused by disease germs.

Each communicable disease is caused by only one kind of germ.

A noncommunicable disease is caused by some other problem within the body and not by disease germs brought into the body.

Some main groups of disease germs are bacteria, viruses, and protozoans.

The body has many defenses against disease germs that enter it.

The body makes a special kind of antibody to fight each kind of disease germ.

For many communicable diseases, having the disease can give a person immunity, or protection against the disease. The disease may confer lifetime immunity, as in the case of chicken pox, or immunity for shorter periods of time.

Vaccines stimulate the body to make protective antibodies against specific communicable disease germs *before* a person becomes infected with these germs.

Because protection from certain vaccines may not last a lifetime, booster doses may be necessary.

[1] See page T43 for Reference Materials related to this chapter.

Behavioral Objectives

See page 170 in the pupil's book where behavioral objectives in the cognitive area are posed directly to pupils.

See also some hoped-for objectives, mainly in the affective area, set forth in the "Teacher's Notes" for page 170.

152–153 *Finding Out About Diseases (Chapter-Opening Pages)*

Use the picture and the text on this page to invite preliminary discussion. Have students use the glossary to answer the question, "What is a disease?"

154 *Preview It*

Make a record of students' own questions about diseases. This list can be added to from time to time as pupils progress through the chapter. You might have the school nurse come in and answer questions not answered in the chapter.

155–156 *What Is a Communicable Disease?*

Review with pupils things they can do to keep from spreading or "catching" disease germs: wash their hands before eating and after using the toilet, cover coughs and sneezes, keep pencils and fingers out of the mouth, use their own towels and washcloths, avoid drinking from a common drinking cup, stay home if they have a cold, and don't get too close to a person with a cold.

157–159 *What Are Some Main Groups of Disease Germs?*

If you have access to a microscope, you may want to let pupils see some slides of different kinds of bacteria. This is a good time to explain how much a microscope can magnify the size of something, and to try to explain how much magnification 1,000 times is.

Mention that most bacteria can be killed by dryness, by sunlight, or by very high temperature. Do pupils know why? The text gives the clue (page 156).

160-162 *How Does the Body Fight Off Disease Germs?*

Point out that pus which sometimes forms around a cut or sore shows in it (when viewed under a microscope) dead white blood cells and dead bacteria. The white cells came to the cut or sore to help fight off disease germs that had entered the skin. Mention that a cut should be washed with soap and water because the soap and water wash some of the germs away.

Explain that while a few harmful disease germs in the body do little harm, *millions* of them can be harmful. And a few disease germs may in 24 hours or so produce many millions more.

163 *Health Around Us*

See what examples students can give of things around them that can help prevent the spread of diseases. For example, there may be a box of paper handkerchiefs in the classroom for covering sneezes and coughs and soap and towels in the washrooms for washing hands.

Have students find out what immunizations they have had and dates of their boosters.

164-165 *Why Do People Still "Catch" Dangerous Diseases?*

An easy way to make a graph that shows how well pupils in a group are protected by immunizations is to give them some colored chalk. Have each child who is immunized against a disease come forward and color in a square on the graph for that disease. Diphtheria, pertussis (whooping cough), and tetanus are grouped together on the graph in the pupil's text because shots for these diseases are usually given together.

This is a good place to mention that chances of catching preventable communicable diseases are increasing because more and more people are failing to get protection for their children and themselves. Childhood diseases have not been wiped out in the U.S. and immunization is needed.

166-167 *Good Health Practices*

Students might make posters about such good health practices as washing a cut with soap and water or staying away from people who have communicable diseases.

168 *Write It*

Be sure to encourage the writing of friendly letters to or the making of get-well cards for classmates who are ill. Put the emphasis on "doing it your own way."

169 *Things to Do*

Another interesting discussion topic concerns what is being done to help improve the health of children around the world. Students themselves may have helped in this effort. Some collected money to buy brood sows and cows to ship to other countries to help people of those countries raise their own protein.

170-173 *Reviews, Tests, School and Home*

Enrichment Suggestions for Chapter 7
Thinking About Community Health[1]

Overview

In Chapter Seven, students learn about important community health, or environmental health, problems. Problems considered include those of air, water, food, and noise pollution; solid waste; litter; and poor housing. Solution of the problems is considered along with their causes. And the role of the health department is clarified.

Important Ideas Developed in the Chapter

People's physical needs include those of air, food, water, and shelter.

The chief responsibility for community health lies with the community health department.

Air pollution is a hazard to health and to property; proper precautions can help reduce it.

A community's water supply can be polluted by untreated or partially treated sewage, by industrial wastes, and by chemicals in soil run-off.

Water pollution can be reduced, in part, by treatment of waste-water and by cleaning of industrial wastes before they are dumped.

Water-treatment plants exist to make community water safe for drinking.

Proper handling and storage of food can help prevent food pollution.

Unsafe housing can endanger the health and safety of those who live in it.

Litter is unsightly and at times unsanitary; it can affect people's feelings of order and well-being.

Some methods available for disposal of solid wastes are more desirable than others.

Imaginative new approaches include burning

[1] See pages T44 and T45 for Reference Materials related to this chapter.

certain garbage and wastes to obtain electricity to heat and light communities.

Too much noise can be harmful to health.

Behavioral Objectives

See page 204 in the pupil's book where behavioral objectives in the cognitive area are posed directly to pupils.

See also some hoped-for objectives, mainly in the affective area, set forth in the "Teacher's Notes" for page 204.

174–175 *Thinking About Community Health* (Chapter-Opening Pages)

Use the questions here to initiate conversation about community health.

You might appoint a committee to gather books about such community health problems as air, water, food, and noise pollution and disposal of solid wastes.

176 *Preview It*

Students may want to try to answer some of the questions posed by titles in this chapter. Do not allot much time for this activity. This section is intended to arouse interest and curiosity.

177–179 *What Does a Health Department Do?*

Have pupils bring in newspaper articles about communities working for a healthful environment. Display the best articles.

180–183 *What Can Be Done About Air Pollution?*

Discuss some things being done at this time. For example, some progress has been made in developing cars and incinerators that produce less pollution.

184-187 *What Can Be Done About Water Pollution?*

Pupils might make simple maps showing the location of their community's water source, the water-treatment plant, and the water-storage towers. Discuss any problems your community may be having with its water supply.

188-190 *What Can Be Done to Prevent Food Pollution?*

You might have volunteers interview food-handlers in food-processing plants, grocery stores, or restaurants. Later they might report back to the group how the food-handlers are trained to help avoid polluting food.

Volunteers might bring in some empty milk cartons for the group to scrutinize. What kind of information is given on the cartons?

191 *Health Around Us*

Have pupils give examples of their community health department in action. Have they seen or heard about a public health nurse making a visit in their neighborhood? What did the nurse do? Have any pupils been immunized in a health-department sponsored program? Against what diseases? Are there signs in the community such as *No Swimming—Polluted Water* or *No Fishing—Polluted Water?* Where are the signs located?

192-193 *What Are Some Housing Problems?*

Invite pupils to bring in pictures from newspapers of any new housing being built in their community. If there are any old buildings being reconstructed or any slum-clearance activities taking place near the school, the class might walk over to see them.

194-195 *What Can Be Done About Litter?*

Ask students why they think litter, junkyards, and even a jumble of neon and other signs in a community are forms of pollution. (Such things are "eyesores"; they spoil the landscape.)

196-199 *Where Will All the Trash and Garbage Go?*

Another problem of solid-waste disposal in every community is what to do with old cars and abandoned cars. Mention that some cities now have "car shredders." These shredders smash metal bodies of cars into small chunks of steel. This steel can be fed directly into furnaces of plants that manufacture new steel products.

200-202 *What Can Be Done About Noise Pollution?*

Discuss the fact that noise is measured in decibels. A whisper is about 20 decibels, ordinary conversation about 60, city noises about 90, a clap of thunder about 110. At 120 decibels, pain begins. At about 140 decibels, the eardrum can break.

A special instrument is used to measure noise. Perhaps you could borrow one from the health department and use it to measure noise levels around the school.

203 *Things to Do*

Pupils might keep track of how often they use water each day. All day long, on a given day, they should jot down every time they use water.

204-212 *Reviews, Tests, School and Home, Bibliographies*

Reference Materials

Chapter One: Getting to Know Yourself and Others

Books for Children

Bunting, Eve. *The Once-A-Year Day*. Childrens Press, 1974. Annie's orphaned cousin comes to live with Annie's family in northern Alaska.

Calhoun, Mary. *Katie John*. Harper, 1960. A lonely girl has to adjust to a new home.

Fassler, Joan. *Howie Helps Himself*. A. Whitman, 1975. An easy-to-read book that will build understanding of the handicapped.

Green, Phyllis. *Ice River*. Addison-Wesley, 1975. An accident on the river brings Dell closer to his stepfather.

Henry, Marguerite. *The Little Fellow*. Rand, 1975. Two foals are used to explore feelings of jealousy between children.

Hoban, Russell. *Dinner at Alberta's*. T. Y. Crowell, 1975. Arthur Crocodile decides to learn table manners when his sister brings a new girl home for supper.

Konigsburg, Elaine L. *Altogether, One at a Time*. Atheneum, 1971. This book has four stories that deal with children's emotions.

LeShan, Eda. *What Makes Me Feel This Way? Growing Up with Human Emotions*. Macmillan, 1972. An excellent first book to help children explore, understand, and enjoy their own feelings.

Livingston, Myra Cohn. *The Way Things Are: And Other Poems*. Atheneum, 1974. Poems for children that reflect young people reacting to the world around them—with questions, doubts, and joy.

Mathis, Sharon Bell. *The Hundred Penny Box*. Viking, 1975. Explores a boy's love for his great-great-aunt who is very old.

Shyer, Marlene Fanta. *Blood in the Snow*. Houghton, 1975. A thought-provoking book that deals with issues of conservation and of a boy's values. For good readers.

Smith, Doris Buchanan. *Kelly's Creek*. T. Y. Crowell, 1975. Kelly's struggle to cope with a learning disability is relieved by his daily visits to a marsh.

Stolz, Mary. *A Dog on Barkham Street*. Harper, 1960. The bully, Martin, spoils the quality of life on Barkham Street.

_____ . *The Bully of Barkham Street*. Harper, 1963. In this book reasons unfold for some of the mean things Martin does.

Warburg, Sandol. *Growing Time*. Houghton, 1969. The death of a pet and a boy's grief are treated with great sensitivity.

White, E. B. *Charlotte's Web*. Harper, 1952. A modern classic with an unusual cast of characters who understand the meaning of love.

Materials for Teachers and Parents[1]

Curwin, Richard L., and Curwin, Geri. *Developing Independent Values in the Classroom*. Education Today, 1974. A practical approach with suggested activities to help children understand who they are, who they'd like to be, and how to become the kind of persons they want to be.

Hawley, Robert C. *Human Values in the Classroom: Teaching for Personal and Social Growth*. Education Research Associates, 1973. Excellent presentation of teaching and learning based on human needs and human values.

_____ . *Value Exploration Through Role Playing*. Hart, 1974. Provides many practical strategies for classroom use of this activity.

Jenkins, Gladys Gardner, and Schacter, Helen S. *These Are Your Children*. 4th ed. Scott, Foresman, 1975. A readable text on child development.

Koch, Kenneth. *Wishes, Lies, and Dreams: Teaching Children to Write Poetry*. Random House, 1971. Gives the teacher classroom-tested approaches to use in helping youngsters enjoy expressing their feelings and experiences through poetry.

Levine, Milton I., and Seligmann, Jean H. *The Parents' Encyclopedia of Infancy, Childhood, and Adolescence*. T. Y. Crowell, 1973. A storehouse of sound, useful information on all aspects of child growth and development.

---

[1] See also specialized reading lists on pages T20, T22, and T24.

Rubin, Louis J. *Facts and Feelings in the Classroom.* Walker, 1973. Excellent for the teacher who wants to create a healthy classroom from the standpoint of mental health.

Films and Filmstrips[2] for Classroom Use
Family Teamwork and You (Aims).

*How Do You Feel? (Imperial).

Let's Share with Others (Coronet).

New Student, New Friends (ABC Media Concepts).

Our Angry Feelings (Perennial, produced by Peshak-Raskin).

*Our Feelings (Scott Education Division).

People (Aims, produced by Films/West).

School Problems: Getting Along with Others (BFA Educational Media).

Chapter Two: Discovering Some Wonders of the Human Body

Books for Children
Adler, Ruth, and Adler, Irving. *Taste, Touch, and Smell.* Day, 1966. Clear explanations are given about three of the five senses.

Bendick, Jeanne. *The Human Senses.* Watts, 1968. Many simple experiments are suggested in this easy-to-read book.

Elgin, Kathleen. *The Skeleton*. Watts, 1970.
_____. *The Muscles.* Watts, 1973.
_____. *The Skin.* Watts, 1970.
Part of a series of reference books entitled *The Human Body.* All are appropriate for most nine- to ten-year-olds.

Goldsmith, Ilse. *Anatomy for Children.* Sterling, 1964. An informative book for advanced readers. Many fascinating details are included.

Perera, Gretchen, and Perera, Thomas. *Your Brain Power.* Coward, 1975. A well-written and humorously illustrated book on the brain and nerves.

Ravielli, Anthony. *Wonders of the Human Body.* Viking, 1954. Eleven printings have been made of this remarkable book. Drawings enhance the text to show the miracle of the human body.

Showers, Paul. *Use Your Brain.* T. Y. Crowell, 1971. A simply-told account of how the brain operates, accompanied by lively illustrations.

_____. *Hear Your Heart.* T. Y. Crowell, 1968.
_____. *A Drop of Blood.* T. Y. Crowell, 1967.
_____. *Your Skin and Mine.* T. Y. Crowell, 1965.
Part of a series of easy books on the human body.

Sullivan, Navin. *Controls in Your Body.* Lippincott, 1971. Information on the controls that keep the body working, even while one sleeps.

White, Anne Terry, and Lietz, Gerald S. *Built to Survive.* Garrard, 1966. Beautifully written book on the magnificence of the human body.

Zim, Herbert S. *Your Brain and How It Works.* Morrow, 1972. Excellent resource material for good readers. See also Zim's book *Bones.*

Material for Teachers and Parents[1]
Byler, Ruth; Lewis, Gertrude; and Totman, Ruth. *Teach Us What We Want to Know.* Published for the Connecticut State Board of Health by the Mental Health Materials Center, 1969. Tells health interests and concerns of children of all ages.

Jones, Kenneth L.; Shainberg, Louis N.; and Byer, Curtis O. *The Human Body.* Harper, 1971. A systematic, illustrated description of each of the systems of the human body.

Nilsson, Lennart. *Behold Man.* Little, Brown, 1974. This book takes the reader on a journey inside the body. Microphotography reveals in a new way the workings of the body. Clear, straightforward text accompanies the remarkable photographs.

Noel, Janet. *The Human Body.* Grosset & Dunlap, 1973. A wealth of pictures and charts makes this visual book a quick reference source.

_____
[1] See also specialized reading lists on pages T20, T22, and T24.
[2] Filmstrips are marked with an asterisk.

Models
Human Skeleton Model. A plastic model of the human skeleton. Model No. 5228 is available, assembled and mounted on a wire stand, from Ideal School Supply, 11000 S. Lavergne Avenue, Oak Lawn, Illinois 60453.

Sensory Models: Eye, Ear, Skin, Nose, and Tongue. Plastic models of the sense organs. Models No. 5220–5224 are available, assembled and painted, from Ideal School Supply (address above).

Films and Filmstrips[2] for Classroom Use
Breathing Easy (American Lung Association).

*Every Body's Skin Makes Everybody Kin (AAHPER and the Institute for Dermatological Communication and Education). Part One and Part Two.

*The Five Senses (Scott Education Division).

*How Do You Know? (Scott Education Division).

Your Body and Its Parts (Britannica Films).

*Your Body Series (Curriculum Materials).

Your Nervous System (Coronet).

Chapter Three: Becoming Safety-Minded

Books for Children
American Red Cross, ed. *Basic First Aid: Books 1, 2, 3, 4.* Doubleday. Series of four easy books of programmed first-aid instruction.

Rinkoff, Barbara. *No Pushing, No Ducking: Safety in the Water.* Lothrop, 1974. Easy-to-read book about hazards in and on the water.

_____. *Red Light Says Stop.* Lothrop, 1974. Easy-to-read, informative introduction to how ideas are communicated without talking.

Material for Teachers and Parents[1]
American National Red Cross. *Advanced First Aid and Emergency Care.* Doubleday, 1973. A good reference for those versed in first aid.

[1] See also specialized reading lists on pages T20, T22, and T24.
[2] Filmstrips are marked with an asterisk.

_____. *Standard First Aid and Personal Safety.* Doubleday, 1973. An invaluable reference. Every library should have a copy.

National Safety Council. Safety Education Data Sheets: *Pedestrian Safety, Swimming, Unauthorized Play Places, Winter Walking.* NSC. Excellent enrichment materials.

_____. *Safety Education Packets.* NSC. These cover such areas as bicycle safety, elementary school safety, and pupil transportation.

_____. *School Safety World.* NSC. A newsletter put out four times a year for teachers.

Thygerson, Alton L. *Safety: Principles, Instruction, and Readings.* Prentice-Hall, 1972. Complete discussion of all aspects of safety education.

U.S. Department of Health, Education, and Welfare. Public Health Service. Food and Drug Administration. *We Want You to Know What We Know About Medicines Without Prescriptions.* DHEW Publication No. (FDA) 73–3009. Up-to-date, extremely useful pamphlet on over-the-counter drugs. Parents will find it interesting.

_____. *We Want You to Know What We Know About Prescription Drugs.* DHEW Publication No. (FDA) 73–3011. Highly readable material reflects recent information on prescription drugs.

Films for Classroom Use
Bicycle Riding Reminders (Aims).

Bicycle Safety (FilmFair Communications).

A Chance to Save a Life (Boy Scouts of America).

Let's Be Safe at Home (Perennial, produced by Portafilms).

Meeting Strangers: Red Light, Green Light (BFA Educational Media).

Playground Safety, 2d ed. (Coronet).

Safe in Recreation (FilmFair Communications).

Safe in the Water (FilmFair Communications).

Safe Living at School, 2d ed. (Coronet).

Safely—Walk to School (Aims).

Safety: Home Safe Home (Aims).

Safety on the Street, 2d ed. (Britannica Films).

Safety with Fire (Coronet).

The Simple Accident (Sid Davis).

Stop, Look and Think (Aims).

Chapter Four: Staying Healthy

Books for Children
Borghese, Anita. *The Down to Earth Cookbook.* Scribner, 1973. This easy-to-use cookbook features natural foods such as whole grain flours and cereals, dried fruits, honey, and nuts. However, recipes involving eggs, milk, cheese, fresh vegetables, meat, and fish are included.

Carr, Rachel E. *Be a Frog, a Bird, or a Tree.* Doubleday, 1973. Children explore movement through mimicry, and are invited to invent their own exercise games.

Hunt, Sarah E. *Games and Sports the World Around.* 3d ed. Ronald, 1964. A fine sourcebook of games children may not have heard of.

Lambie, Laurie Jo. *Daisy Discovers Dance.* Day, 1973. Two children explore movement—animal movements, geometric shapes, letters, colors. Delightful, full-color illustrations add to the book's excitement.

Paul, Aileen. *Kids Cooking Complete Meals: Menus, Recipes, Instructions.* Doubleday, 1975. International and regional menus are a feature of this book for the more advanced student.

Paul, Aileen, and Hawkins, Arthur. *Kids Cooking: A First Cookbook for Children.* Doubleday, 1971. A practical book for beginners. All the dishes featured are well-established favorites.

Shay, Arthur. *What It's Like to Be a Nurse.* Reilly & Lee, 1972. Photographic account of student nurses in training. Another informative book by the same author is *What It's Like to Be a Doctor.*

Showers, Paul. *Sleep Is for Everyone.* T. Y. Crowell, 1974. An easy-to-read reference book packed with fascinating information.

_____. *What Happens to a Hamburger.* T. Y. Crowell, 1970. Good explanation of how our bodies make use of the things we eat. Easy.

Woolley, Catherine. *Ginnie and Geneva Cookbook.* Morrow, 1975. Collection of recipes suitable for nine- to twelve-year-olds. Aimed at girls.

Materials for Teachers and Parents[1]
Bedeschi, Giulio. *Science of Medicine.* Watts, 1975. Covers the development of medical science from Hippocrates to the Houston Space Center. Good reference may appeal to advanced students.

Bogert, L. Jean, and others. *Nutrition and Physical Fitness.* 9th ed. Saunders, 1973. Basic sourcebook for nutrition information.

Boston Children's Medical Center and Feinbloom, Richard I. *Child Health Encyclopedia.* Delacorte, 1975. A wealth of material on all aspects of child growth and development. Written and indexed for use by parents.

Fabricius, Helen. *Physical Education for the Classroom Teacher.* 2d ed. W. C. Brown, 1971. Extremely helpful for those not trained in physical education.

Films and Filmstrips[2] for Classroom Use
Alcohol: A New Focus (American Educational Films).

Busy Bodies (Stanton).

Cleanliness and Health, 2d ed. (Coronet).

Dance Your Own Way (BFA Educational Media).

Exploring Your Growth (Churchill).

Food, Energy, and You (Perennial, produced by Wexler).

Food Preservation (Aims, produced by Films/West).

---

[1] See also specialized reading lists on pages T20, T22, and T24.
[2] Filmstrips are marked with an asterisk.

Health Helpers (Britannica Films).

Physical Education—Basic Skills (Aims). Series of two films.

Project AM (Cereal Institute).

Smoking: A New Focus (American Educational Films).

Something You Didn't Eat (Walt Disney).

What's Good to Eat? (Perennial, produced by Wexler).

Why Exercise? (Aims).

Chapter Five: Learning About Teeth

Books for Children
Barr, George. *Young Scientist and the Dentist.* McGraw-Hill, 1970. A highly informative reference book for good readers.

Hammond, Winifred G. *The Riddle of Teeth.* Coward, 1971. A simply written book full of answers to children's often asked questions.

Lapp, Carolyn. *Dentists' Tools.* Lerner, 1961. Offers interesting details about the various tools and kinds of equipment a dentist uses.

Shay, Arthur. *What It's Like to Be a Dentist.* Reilly & Lee, 1972. Large photographs and easy-to-read text make this a popular reference book on the work of the dentist and on dentistry as a career.

Materials for Teachers and Parents[1]
American Dental Association. *Cleaning Your Teeth and Gums* and *Happiness Is a Healthy Mouth.* ADA. Basic, up-to-date information on flossing and brushing teeth provided in two booklets.

The Bureau of Dental Health Education of the American Dental Association has available, at low cost, many dental health teaching kits, pamphlets, and posters. Write to the Bureau at the ADA, 211 E. Chicago Avenue, Chicago, Illinois 60611 for a catalog.

[1] See also specialized reading lists on pages T20, T22, and T24.

Garfield, Sydney. *Teeth, Teeth, Teeth.* Simon & Schuster, 1971. A useful reference book that also contains welcome touches of humour.

National Institutes of Health: Division of Dental Health, National Institute of Dental Research. *Tooth Care.* DHEW Publication (NIH) 73–449.

Model
Giant Tooth: A plastic model, hinged to show interior structure of a molar. Model No. 5230 is available, assembled and painted, from Ideal School Supply, 11000 S. Lavergne Avenue, Oak Lawn, Illinois 60453.

Films for Classroom Use
Dental Health: How and Why (Coronet).

The Haunted Mouth (American Dental Association).

The Munchers: A Fable (American Dental Association).

Showdown at Sweet Rock Gulch (American Dental Association).

Teeth Are for Keeping (American Dental Association).

Chapter Six: Finding Out About Diseases

Books for Children
Frahm, Anne. *The True Book of Bacteria.* Childrens Press, 1963. A very easy book, but one that gives much information.

Goldsmith, Ilse. *Why You Get Sick and How You Get Well.* Sterling, 1970. An excellent reference source for good readers.

Lewis, Lucia. *Microbes.* Rev. ed. Watts, 1972. Advanced readers will find this book useful.

Lietz, Gerald S. *Bacteria.* Garrard, 1964. A Junior Science Book. Long a favorite with fourth-graders.

Selsam, Millicent E. *Gregg's Microscope.* Harper, 1963. A Science-I-Can-Read book. Reluctant readers will enjoy it and might use it as the basis of reports on how a microscope helps us.

Materials for Teachers and Parents[1]
Aylesworth, Thomas G. *The World of Microbes.*
Watts, 1975. The story of the growth of micro-
biology from hobby to science. Good reference.
Might appeal to advanced students.

Boston Children's Medical Center and Feinbloom,
Richard I. *Child Health Encyclopedia.* Delacorte,
1975. Alphabetical listing of childhood illnesses and
diseases. Written and indexed for use by parents.

Donahue, Parnell, and Capellaro, Helen. *Germs
Make Me Sick!* Knopf, 1975. Good reference book
with cartoon illustrations. Covers a wide variety of
diseases and their treatments.

Dubos, René. *The Unseen World.* Rockefeller, 1962.
A readable, well-illustrated book by one of the
country's leading scientists.

Rosebury, Theodor. *Life on Man.* Viking, 1969.
A highly interesting book that offers good background for this chapter.

Schneider, Leo. *Microbes in Your Life.* Harcourt,
1966. You will find information in this book suitable for passing on to your students.

Source for Microbe-Growing Materials
Turtox Biological Supply House, 8200 S. Hoyne
Avenue, Chicago, Illinois 60620, or any other
scientific supply house.

Films and Filmstrips[2] **for Classroom Use**
Bacteriology—Louis Pasteur and Robert Koch
(Scott Education Division). From the *Great Discov-
eries in Science* series.

Cleanliness and Health, 2d ed. (Coronet).

Health—Communicable Diseases (Aims, produced by
Cahill).

Health Habits Series (Curriculum Materials).

Health Heroes—The Battle Against Disease (Coronet).

---

[1] See also specialized reading lists on pages T20, T22,
and T24.
[2] Filmstrips are marked with an asterisk.

Health in Balance (Perennial, produced by Weisen-
born).

How to Catch a Cold (Walt Disney).

Microbes and Their Control (BFA Educational
Media).

Your Protection Against Disease (Britannica Films).

Chapter Seven: Thinking About Community Health

Books for Children
Beame, Rona. *What Happens to Garbage.* Messner,
1975. Discusses the means used by New York City
to collect and dispose of refuse.

Bloome, Enid. *The Air We Breathe!* Doubleday,
1971. A very easy book about how air gets polluted
and what an individual can do about it.

Elliott, Sarah M. *Our Dirty Air.* Messner, 1971.
Good discussion of air pollution and how it affects
human, plant, and animal life.

_____. *Our Dirty Water.* Messner, 1973.
Good discussion of water pollution.

Kalina, Sigmund. *Three Drops of Water.* Lothrop,
1974. Follows the path of three drops of water from
the top of a mountain down to the sea in a study of
water pollution.

Leaf, Munro. *Who Cares? I Do.* Lippincott, 1971.
Easy-to-read book about spoilers of our environment
—especially the droppers and wreckers.

Pringle, Laurence. *City and Suburb.* Macmillan,
1975. Well-illustrated book describes the city-suburb
ecosystem.

Radlauer, Edward, and Radlauer, Ruth S. *Water for
Your Community.* Childrens Press, 1968. How communities manage their water supplies.

Shanks, Ann Zane. *About Garbage and Stuff.*
Viking, 1973. A good introduction to the concept
and processes of recycling.

Showers, Paul. *Where Does the Garbage Go?* T. Y. Crowell, 1974. Explains what happens to garbage once it has been dumped—where it goes and how it could be used. Easy.

Shuttlesworth, Dorothy E., and Cervasio, Thomas. *Litter—The Ugly Enemy.* Doubleday, 1973. Good emphasis on how the problem of solid wastes is being slowly conquered by scientists, technicians, and private citizens. Advanced.

Smaridge, Norah. *Litterbugs Come in Every Size.* Golden Press, 1972. Simple but intriguing discussion of litter.

Tannenbaum, Beulah, and Stillman, Myra. *Clean Air.* McGraw-Hill, 1974. Discusses city, industrial, and individual contributions to air pollution, its harmful effects, and progress being made to achieve cleaner air.

Materials for Teachers and Parents[1]
Hilton, Suzanne. *How Do They Get Rid of It?* Westminster, 1970. Junior-high reference book that elementary teachers will find useful.

Marshall, James. *Going to Waste: Where Will All the Garbage Go?* Coward, 1972. Another book for junior–senior high school that offers helpful information about solid waste disposal.

Miles, Betty. *Save the Earth! An Ecology Handbook for Kids.* Knopf, 1974. A valuable handbook for teachers and parents, rich with explanations, photographs, songs, poems, and suggested experiments. May appeal to advanced students.

Films and Filmstrips[2] for Classroom Use
Conservation—A Job for Young America (McGraw-Hill).

Ee-Yi-Ee-Yi-Oh (Perennial, produced by Portafilms).

Health—You and Your Helpers (Aims).

Noise (BFA Educational Media, produced by Don Dickerson).

Our Part in Conservation (McGraw-Hill).

Problems of Conservation: Air (Britannica Films).

Problems of Conservation: Water (Britannica Films).

Water and How We Use It (Coronet).

Workers for the Public Welfare (Eye Gate House).

[1] See also specialized reading lists on pages T20, T22, and T24.
[2] Filmstrips are marked with an asterisk.

Student Questionnaire *You and Your Health*

How do you like your *Health* book?
I like it very much ☐¹   It's O.K. ☐²   I don't like it ☐³

How easy is it for you to read?
Just right ☐¹   Too easy ☐²   Too hard ☐³

What would you say about the pictures in the *Health* book?
Help me a lot ☐¹   Help me sometimes ☐²   Don't help me ☐³

What parts of the *Health* book do you like?

☐¹ The body and how it works   ☐⁸ Health careers
☐² Care of the body   ☐⁹ How you grow
☐³ Diseases and germs   ☐¹⁰ Medical advances
☐⁴ Drugs including alcohol and tobacco ☐¹¹ Safety and first aid
☐⁵ Ecology and pollution   ☐¹² Teeth
☐⁶ Exercise and sleep   ☐¹³ Understanding others
☐⁷ Foods   ☐¹⁴ Understanding yourself

What special sections of the *Health* book do you like?

☐¹ Can You Show What You Know?   ☐⁵ School and Home
☐² Enjoy It   ☐⁶ Tell It
☐³ Health Around Us   ☐⁷ Things to Do
☐⁴ Safety Around Us   ☐⁸ Write It

If there are any other parts of the *Health* book you liked, write them below.

Scott, Foresman and Company   1900 East Lake Avenue   Glenview, Illinois 60025

Teacher's Questionnaire *You and Your Health*

Please complete this questionnaire after you have finished teaching the **new** Scott, Foresman HEALTH Program for the school year. Remove the questionnaire from the book, fold it as shown, staple it, and place it in the nearest mailbox. No postage is required.

1. How would you identify the overall ability of the children in your class?

    EMH or TMH ☐   Below average ☐   Average ☐   Above average ☐   Gifted ☐

2. Was the text an effective teaching tool? Why or why not? _____

    _____

    _____

3. What is your opinion of the readability? _____

    _____

4. How useful are the illustrations in helping students learn? _____

    _____

5. Did any parts of the text cause learner difficulty? _____

    _____

    _____

6. What improvements would you suggest? _____

    _____

    _____

7. What health questions do your pupils ask most often? _____

    _____

    _____

8. Indicate which features of the text you like and which features you do not like.

Like	Don't Like		Like	Don't Like	
☐	☐	Chapter-Opening Pages	☐	☐	Things to Do
☐	☐	Preview It	☐	☐	Can You Show What You Know?
☐	☐	Enjoy It	☐	☐	Review It
☐	☐	Write It	☐	☐	Chapter Test
☐	☐	Health Around Us	☐	☐	School and Home
				☐	Special Research

9. Indicate which features of the Teacher's Edition you like and which features you do not like.

Like	Don't Like		Like	Don't Like	
☐	☐	Teacher's Notes	☐	☐	A Healthful Classroom Environment
☐	☐	Family-Life Education	☐	☐	Signs and Symptoms of Illness
☐	☐	Enrichment Suggestions	☐	☐	The Parent-Teacher Conference
☐	☐	Reference Materials	☐	☐	If Children Ask About Death
☐	☐	A Developmental Profile of	☐	☐	Movement Exploration and Games
☐	☐	Nine- to Ten-Year-Olds	☐	☐	The "How" of Health Teaching

If you would be willing to complete a questionnaire after teaching the program for another year, please fill in your return address.

Name _____

School _____

Address _____

City _____ State _____ Zip Code _____

Fold on dotted line so return address and mailing address are on outside of questionnaire.

FIRST CLASS
PERMIT No. 282
GLENVIEW, ILL.

POSTAGE WILL BE PAID BY

SCOTT, FORESMAN AND COMPANY
LEARNER VERIFICATION DEPT.
1900 EAST LAKE AVENUE
GLENVIEW, ILLINOIS 60025

School, Home, Community **You and Your Health**

Julius B. Richmond, M.D.
Elenore T. Pounds, M.A.

In consultation with
Orvis A. Harrelson, M.D., M.P.H.
Gladys Gardner Jenkins, M.A.
Dieter H. Sussdorf, Ph.D.
Wallace Ann Wesley, Hs.D.

Scott, Foresman and Company
Glenview, Illinois

Dallas, Texas Palo Alto, California
Oakland, New Jersey Tucker, Georgia

Authors

Julius B. Richmond, M.D. Professor of Child Psychiatry and Human Development and Professor and Chairman, Department of Social and Preventive Medicine, Harvard Medical School; Director, Judge Baker Guidance Center; Chief of Psychiatric Service, Children's Hospital Medical Center, Boston, Massachusetts.

Elenore T. Pounds, M.A. Writer; lecturer; former Directing Editor of the Health and Personal Development Program; classroom teacher; coauthor of the *Health and Growth* Program; author of *Drugs and Your Safety* and other *Health Enrichment Booklets*.

Consultants

Orvis A. Harrelson, M.D., M.P.H. Corporate Medical Director, Weyerhauser Company, Tacoma, Washington; former Administrative Director of Health, Tacoma Public Schools, Tacoma, Washington.

Gladys Gardner Jenkins, M.A. Lecturer in Parent-Child-Teacher Relationships, University of Iowa, Iowa City, Iowa; former member, National Advisory Council on Child Growth and Human Development; author of *Helping Children Reach Their Potential;* coauthor of *These Are Your Children*.

Dieter H. Sussdorf, Ph.D. Associate Professor of Microbiology, Cornell University Graduate School of Medical Sciences, New York, New York; coauthor of *Methods in Immunology*.

Wallace Ann Wesley, Hs.D. Director, Department of Health Education, American Medical Association, Chicago, Illinois; former teacher at primary through college levels.

ISBN: 0–673–11013–3

ISBN: 0–673–11005–2

2345678910-RRC-85848382818079787776

Content Specialists

Richard H. Blum, Ph.D. Consulting Professor, Department of Psychology and Director, Joint Program in Drugs, Crime, and Community Studies, Center for Interdisciplinary Research, Stanford University, Stanford, California.

Willie D. Ford, Ph.D. Professor, Nutrition and Home Economics, Grambling State University, Grambling, Louisiana; former Nutrition Specialist, U.S. Department of Agriculture, University of Nebraska, Lincoln, Nebraska.

Lucia Guzman, B.S. Assistant to the Dean for Student Affairs, University of Texas School of Allied Health Sciences, University of Texas Medical Branch, Galveston, Texas.

Barbara J. Kohuth, B.S. Environmental Health Educator; Head, Office of Environmental Education and Public Information, Cleveland Department of Public Health and Welfare, Cleveland, Ohio.

Boyd T. Marsh, M.A., B.S. Deputy Health Commissioner for Environmental Health, Cleveland Department of Public Health and Welfare, Cleveland, Ohio.

Norman H. Olsen, D.D.S. Chairman of the Department of Pedodontics and Dean of The Dental School, Northwestern University, Chicago, Illinois.

Marguerite Robinson, M.S. Consumer Specialist, Department of Health, Education, Welfare, Food and Drug Administration, Chicago, Illinois; Past President, Chicago Nutrition Association, Chicago, Illinois.

Joan Tillotson, Ph.D. Consultant in Movement Education, The University of North Carolina at Charlotte, Charlotte, North Carolina.

Wilma Yee, B.S., R.N. Public Health Nurse and School Nurse, Oakland Public Schools, Oakland, California.

The assistance of the National Safety Council, Chicago, Illinois, in reviewing the safety advice in this material is gratefully acknowledged.

Learner Feedback

Experimental versions of many of the lessons in the YOU AND YOUR HEALTH Program for grade four were used during the 1975–1976 school year with students at Fern-Greenwood Elementary School, Torrance, California; Ruth N. Upson Elementary School, Jacksonville, Florida; and Public School 276, Brooklyn, New York. The authors and editors of the program are grateful to the students and to the teachers in these schools for their comments and their suggestions.

Teacher's Notes

In this *Teacher's Edition* "Teacher's Notes" are overprinted on the pupil's pages.
With the exception of specialized health and safety words, this book uses most of the vocabulary words found in well-known vocabulary lists for third-grade and early fourth-grade levels. The pupil's text has been kept easy so that all nine- to ten-year-olds can enjoy health and safety material "custom built" for their special health needs and interests.

Contents

1 Getting to Know Yourself and Others

What do you know about yourself? What might you *not* know? What would you like to learn more about?

Now think about the others in your group. Do you really know most of them? Or do you just know many of them by name? How might you get to know others in your group better?

9

Teacher's Notes
See the Enrichment Suggestions for
Chapter One on pages T25–T26 of the
Teacher's Supplement. See also
suggested Reference Materials on page
T39.
"Preview It" is a special feature that
occurs at the beginning of each
chapter in this book and in this health
series. Here students do some
anticipating. They skim over the main
headings in the chapter. Most of these
headings are, by design, study
questions. Curiosities are aroused, and
pupils are given a framework for the
detailed information to follow.
See also page T25 for additional
teaching suggestions.

Preview It

Do you ever look in the looking-glass
And see a stranger there?
A child you know and do not know,
Wearing what you wear?

Everyone feels like a stranger to himself or herself now and then. This chapter should help you get to know yourself better. And it should also help you learn more about others.

You probably know that no one is exactly the same as you. But do you know that you are *like* others in many ways too?

For example, most people want to be noticed now and then. Everyone wants to be liked and to have friends. And everyone has feelings too. Sometimes the feelings are pleasant. But sometimes they aren't. When our feelings are unpleasant, we wonder what to do.

Look quickly through this chapter. What questions do the main titles ask about you and others? Which questions make you curious? What other questions do you have? Where might you find the answers?

What Is Special About You?

Suppose you are in a group like the one you see here. Some of you know each other. But most of you don't.

Then each of you is given a name tag. Now you know the name of everyone in the group. But you still don't know very much about the others, do you?

Teacher's Notes
Use the title question to find out how students identify themselves. Then have students study the page to see if a person's name is enough to help others get to know him or her. If not, what other ways might there be to become acquainted with someone? Now have pupils study pages 12 and 13. On these pages they learn some ways in which they can share their interests and concerns with others. See also page T25.

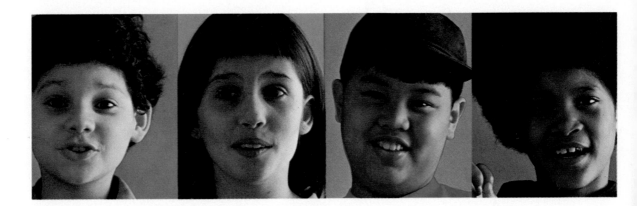

Now suppose you are given a short time to plan how to help others get to know you better.

You might plan a short talk about yourself. You might draw a picture or write about something you like to do. Perhaps you might act out a game or sport you like to play.

Whatever you choose to do, your job is to help others get to know you better.

What would you do? Think about it. Then turn the page and read on.

"I collect shells. So far I have about fourteen different kinds. This is a picture of one of my shells. Do you know what kind of shell it is?"

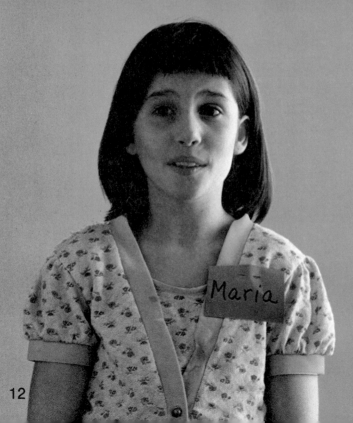

"My name is Maria Peters. And I am new at this school. My family just moved here from Dallas, Texas.

"We are going to get a dog. Do you know anyone who has puppies to give away?"

Here are the same boys and girls that you saw on page 11. Do you know them better now? Why?

How can you help Maria? What might you ask Eduardo to do?

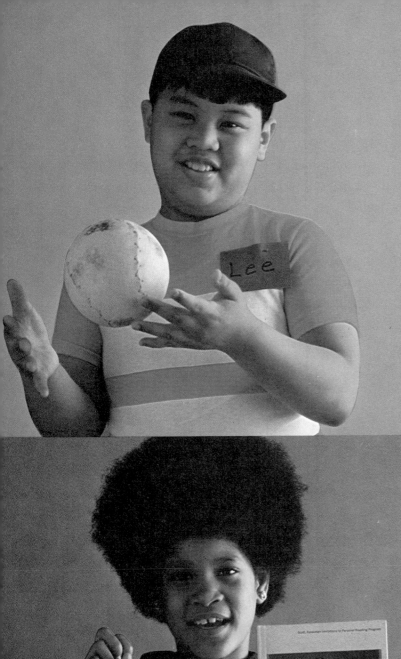

"You can guess what I like to do most of all. I play this game all the time. At home I watch the game on TV. The *Green Sox* are my favorite team."

"I love to read. My favorite books right now are the Eddie books. I've read *Annie Pat and Eddie* and *Little Eddie.* Now I've started *Eddie and Gardenia.* All the Eddie books are really funny."

What might you ask Lee? What could you talk to Peggy about?

Now you might try to help others in your group get to know *you* better. How could this activity help?

13

Teacher's Notes
This activity offers an easy way to reassure children that they share many experiences and emotions with others in their group.
(*Note:* Special features in the margin, such as "Something to Do," are designed to keep children active, interested, and alert throughout each chapter.)
See also page T26 for additional teaching suggestions.

How Are You Like Others?

You've learned some ways in which you and others are special. Now here's a way to find out how you are *like* others in your group.

Your teacher is going to read the statements below aloud. If a statement applies to you, raise your hand. Look around the room. How many others have raised their hands too?

I have a pet.
My grandmother or grandfather lives with me.
I am the oldest in the family.
I am the youngest in the family.
I am the only child in the family.
I am afraid of lightning.
I watch cartoons on TV on Saturday morning.
I have been in a bus.
I have moved several times.
My brother or sister sometimes makes me angry.
My mother works away from home.
I have a secret hiding place.
I often make my own breakfast.
I feel scared when I have to give a report.
I have a library card.
I know how to swim.
I have had a ride in an airplane.
I have "scary" dreams sometimes.
I have a favorite color.
I help at home.
I like to ride my bike.
I feel lonely sometimes.

What can you learn from this activity?

Something to Do

Think of something you like to do. Do you collect stamps? Do you play baseball? Do you read books about horses?

See if you can find someone else in your group who likes to do the same things you do. Who is it? What do you both like to do?

Adapted by special permission from *Developing Individual Values in the Classroom* by Richard and Geri Curwin. © 1974 by Education Today Company, Inc., 530 University Avenue, Palo Alto, California 94301.

What Makes People Likeable?

Brenda is feeling left out of things. "Nobody seems to care that I'm here all by myself," she is thinking.

Then Brenda thought of a question.

Why aren't some people liked as well as other people?

Think about that question. Have some answers ready. Then turn the page and read on.

Teacher's Notes
Use the picture and caption here to initiate preliminary discussion. Then have students compare their ideas with the ones on page 16.

Some people do things that annoy others. People who often do annoying things are not well liked. But people who are liked usually do likeable and friendly things.

Two imaginary children are shown below.

Robin often does things that annoy others. People do not like Robin very much. What are some things Robin does to annoy others? What else can you add to the list?

Pat often does things that make others feel friendly. People like Pat. What does Pat do to make people like her? What other things can you add to the list?

Robin makes fun of people.

Robin always wants to be first in line.

Robin talks to you one day and not the next.

Robin laughs if you make a mistake.

Robin always wants to win.

Robin brags a lot.

Pat shares things with others.

Pat gives you help if you need it.

Pat says nice things like, "What game would you like to play?"

Pat always tries to keep promises.

Pat takes turns.

Books to Read

Look in your school or public library for these books:

Stolz, Mary. *A Dog on Barkham Street* (Harper). Find out about a boy who did things that others did not like. What things did the boy do that bothered others?

Stolz, Mary. *The Bully of Barkham Street* (Harper). Find out why the bully of Barkham Street did things to annoy others. Why do you think people sometimes do things that others do not like?

What Can You Do About Scared Feelings?

Andy has a problem. Today he is supposed to give a report at school.

He is feeling scared and shy. He wants to give the report. But he is also afraid.

What do you think he should do?

Read the next page. Compare your ideas with the ones given there.

Teacher's Notes
Use the picture and caption to initiate preliminary discussion. Then have pupils compare their ideas with the ones on page 18.

17

Andy is having mixed feelings or *emotions.* He wants to give his report to the group. Yet he feels a little scared.

Everyone feels scared now and then. Scared feelings often come when we are learning to do new things. Or they may come when we are trying to do things we think we cannot do very well.

What can Andy do about his feelings? And what can you do about scared feelings?

Sometimes it helps to talk about your scared or shy feelings with someone. Talk to your mother or father, your teacher, an older brother or sister, or a friend.

But most of the time it helps to go ahead and try doing the thing that scares you. Many times your scared or shy feelings go away. Andy, for example, might find that his scared feelings would disappear once he started his report.

Once you find the courage to do what you fear doing, you will feel better. You may even feel a little proud and surprised when things turn out so well. Next time it will become easier to do the thing you fear.

Of course, there are times when you really should be scared. For example, you should always be afraid to take an unsafe dare. Sometimes being afraid can help keep you and others safe.

Think of a time when you felt scared or shy. What did you do? What would you do now?

Teacher's Notes

Help students summarize useful things they have learned about dealing with scared or shy feelings. Emphasize that everyone feels shy or scared at times. Each child might also write a summary of the lesson by copying and completing this sentence:

When you are scared or shy, it often helps. . . .

Glossary word: *emotion*

See also page T26 for additional teaching suggestions.

Something to Remember

Sometimes you feel a little shy when you meet a stranger, especially a grown-up. It helps if you know what to do and say.

Try to look at the stranger. Then smile and say, "How do you do." You might also want to shake hands with the person.

People also like to be called by name. So you might say, "Hello, Dr. Bell."

What Can You Do About Angry Feelings?

Susan is very angry with her little brother Tommy. Tommy has broken part of a game that belongs to Susan.

What do you think Susan should do?

What might help Susan get over her angry feelings?

Read the next page. Compare your ideas with the ones given there.

Teacher's Notes
Use the picture and caption to initiate preliminary discussion. Then have students compare their ideas with the ones on page 20.

19

Susan is feeling angry. We all feel angry when something we own has been broken.

Sometimes we feel angry when we think we have been treated unfairly. Or we may feel angry when we think we are being left out of things. At times it is hard to get over our angry feelings.

What can Susan do about her angry feelings? And what can you do about such feelings?

You might try talking things over, instead of hitting or hurting others. Susan, for example, could tell Tommy why she is angry. Susan might also talk with the rest of her family. They could give her some good ideas about other places to keep her toys.

Talking over your angry feelings is better than keeping them locked up inside you. As long as the angry feelings are inside, you will feel upset and unhappy.

If there is nobody around to talk with, do something else for a while. Doing other things will help until you have a chance to talk about your feelings. You can see a list of things you might try at the right.

What has made you angry lately? What did you do about it? What would you do now?

Sum It Up

How can you get to know others better?

What are some ways you are like others?

What makes a person likeable? What can make a person not-so-likeable?

What can help when you feel scared or angry?

Teacher's Notes

Point out that sometimes our angry feelings pass quickly. But when angry feelings stay with us for a while, we should try to get rid of them. Help students discuss what they might do to get rid of angry feelings. Students might also try to write a paragraph, using this sentence as a starter:

Once I felt angry when. . . .

Later you might read aloud some of the unsigned paragraphs and discuss (a) how the person felt, (b) who or what made the person feel that way, and (c) what might be done about the feelings.

(*Note:* "Sum It Up" is a feature that occurs at intervals throughout each chapter of this book and of others in this health series. Pupils can use this study aid to review important ideas learned in the preceding pages.)

See also page T26 for additional teaching suggestions.

Something to Try

Here is a list of things you might try when you are feeling angry:

Play a game outside with friends.

Read a book.

Watch an interesting TV program.

Draw a picture about how angry you feel.

Call a friend on the telephone.

20

ENJOY IT

Teacher's Notes
A special attempt is made in this health series to enrich children's lives by exposing them to poetry and to art that is related to the lesson topics. Here students have a chance to enjoy a poem about feelings.
Encourage them to find other poems about feelings. Read the poems in class or post them on the bulletin board.
See page T26 for additional teaching suggestions.

Lemons and Apples

One day I might feel
Mean.
And squinched up inside,
Like a mouth sucking on a
Lemon.

The next day I could
Feel
Whole and happy
And right.
Like an unbitten apple.

How do you feel today?
Why do you think you feel as you do?

From *Woody and Me,* by Mary Neville, illustrated by Ronnie Solbert. Copyright © 1966 by Mary Neville Woodrich and Ronnie Solbert. Reprinted by permission of Pantheon Books, a Division of Random House, Inc., and Mary Neville (Woodrich).

Teacher's Notes

Research indicates that children from about age six to nine are experimenting with alcohol and tobacco at an increasing rate. Research also indicates that the command, "Don't!" is effective with this age group. The command is especially effective if it comes from a credible authority, such as a doctor or a parent.

Youngsters often start experimenting with alcohol or tobacco because others they know are doing it. Children this age usually know that such substances are harmful. But the problem is one of peer pressure. In other words, a child may be afraid to say "no" for fear of being disliked or losing friends.

Pages 22–24 should help children face situations where there is pressure from others of their own age, or a little older. The lesson points out that a person doesn't have to do what others are doing when he or she knows it is harmful.

Do You Have to Do What Others Are Doing?

Dick Banta had a hard time when his family moved. Not many boys lived near Dick. He missed having someone to play with after school.

Then one afternoon a boy from his class named Paul stopped him. Paul said, "You live near me. Let's walk home together."

Dick was very pleased. It was great to have a friend.

On the way home, Dick and Paul met another boy named Jake. He seemed to know Paul.

"Say there," said Jake. "I have something you might like to try. Have a little puff. You'll like it."

"Well," said Paul. "I don't know. Maybe I'll try it."

"Oh," thought Dick. "I don't want to try that cigarette. But what will Paul think if I don't? Should I or shouldn't I?"

Something to Do

You might have a member of your group write to the American Cancer Society (219 East 42nd Street, New York, New York 10017). Ask for free material about the way smoking can affect health. Post the material on your bulletin board.

One day you may have a problem like Dick has. Your friends may want you to do things that you think are unsafe or wrong. Then you may feel confused and unsure about what to do.

Try to decide what you think Dick should do. Then turn the page and read on.

Teacher's Notes
Use the picture and story to initiate preliminary discussion. Then have students compare their ideas with the ones on page 24.

Below are some things that boys and girls your age said in talking about Dick's problem. You can also read what their teacher said.

Diane: Dick's problem is whether to do something he knows he shouldn't do. I think he knows it's harmful to smoke cigarettes.

Ray: Sure he does. Just like he knows that he shouldn't take a drink with *alcohol* in it. Some fellow tried to get me to take a drink. I said, "No!"

Patti: Dick has another problem too. He's afraid that Paul might get mad if he doesn't try that cigarette.

Jill: I don't think he should do that. If he doesn't want to smoke he should say so. Nobody is making him smoke.

Louis: Maybe Paul doesn't know that smoking can be harmful. Dick could say, "We have to go home now." On the way home he could explain.

Ms. Hernandez: Dick's problem is one we all have at times. Should you do something just because others are doing it? Or should you have enough courage to do what you think is right? Dick knows that smoking can be harmful. I think he'll have the courage to politely say, "No, I don't want to smoke."

What would *you* do if you were Dick?

What hard decisions have you made lately? What might you do differently?

Teacher's Notes

Emphasize that it is possible to politely refuse such things as a cigarette and an alcoholic beverage. Later you may want to expand the discussion to include some of the harmful effects of tobacco and alcohol.

Smoking, for example, makes the heart work harder. Smoking can also be a factor in causing such diseases as lung cancer and emphysema (in which the lungs lose their capacity to work properly). Emphasize that once started, smoking is a difficult habit to break.

(*Note:* When young children smoke, they may become nervous, perform poorly in school, and have less-than-adequate adjustment in other areas of living.)

Point out that alcohol is a drug. It can have unexpected and dangerous effects, especially on children. Even a small amount of alcohol affects the way the brain works. After drinking an alcoholic beverage, a person cannot reason or make judgments as well as usual. And children can become extremely ill from an overdose of alcohol.

Glossary word: *alcohol*

See also page T26.

Something to Think About

What are some times when you might have to choose between doing what others are doing or taking a stand for what you think is right? Try to act out what you would do or say.

What Can Help When a Pet Dies?

Janet was crying on the school playground one morning.

Before long, some friends found out what was wrong. Janet's pet cat, Fuzzy, had died that morning. Janet was feeling sad and lonely. She kept saying, "I want Fuzzy back."

What do you think Janet's friends might do or say to help? Now turn the page and read on.

Teacher's Notes
Before beginning this lesson, you might want to read the article, "If Children Ask About Death" on pages T23 and T24 of the Teacher's Supplement. Then use the picture and caption to initiate preliminary discussion. Have students compare their ideas with the ones on page 26.

Here are some things Janet's friends did and said:

Susan: Go ahead and cry, Janet. We know how you feel. When our dog died, everyone in the family cried.

Sara: Janet, that's too bad. I'm so sorry.

Bill: I'm sorry too. Sure you want Fuzzy back.

Lee: But Fuzzy can't come back. Fuzzy is dead. That means she isn't living any more.

Susan: But even if Fuzzy is dead, Janet can remember her. She can keep a part of Fuzzy "alive in her head." That's what my mother said when our dog died.

Tony: That's right, Janet. You can think of all the fun you used to have with Fuzzy.

Sara: Let's go in early and tell our teacher. He'll want to know about it, Janet. And he'll want to know why you are feeling sad today.

Which ideas do you think will help Janet the most?

Did you ever have a pet that died? What did you do that helped you then?

If you once had a pet, is part of it still "alive in your head"? What are some happy memories you have of your pet?

Sum It Up

Should you always do something because others are doing it? Why or why not?

What are some things that can help when a pet dies?

Teacher's Notes

Teachers have asked for help in dealing with the subject of death. So this lesson focuses on an experience common to many children—the death of a pet.

Students can participate in the discussion according to the level of their interest and ability. Many children will merely want to listen. You may also want to emphasize some of the following ideas:

It's natural to cry when a pet dies.

It's helpful for others to say, "I'm sorry."

A pet that has died is not going to return to life and that fact must be accepted.

We can remember our pets and recall happy times we have had with them.

It helps to talk with others about our feelings of sorrow.

Some students may offer comments such as, "Janet's pet has gone to heaven." Others may disagree. Your role is to point out that different people have different beliefs. Not everything is known about death. It is still a mystery in many ways.

See also page T26 for additional teaching suggestions.

A Book to Read

You might look in the library for this book.

Warburg, Sandol. *Growing Time* (Houghton). The story is about a boy whose much-loved dog dies. A new puppy helps the boy get over his sadness.

WRITE IT

Do colors give you special feelings, such as happiness or sadness? Sometimes you can show how you feel about something by writing about it.

Here is what one child your age wrote about colors. What can you write?

Teacher's Notes

Another feature of this health book and of others in the series is the recurring use of writings by children. Exposure to such writings offers students an opportunity to do some creative writing of their own.

If students need help writing a poem or paragraph about colors, you might offer these suggestions:

A color that makes me feel happy is, . . .

A color I think of as an angry color is . . . because. . . .

See also page T26.

Colors Are a Feeling

Red makes me feel like sunshine shining on a hill.

Blue doesn't look like red. Blue makes the day seem dull.

Pink doesn't make me feel like sunshine. Pink unlike red makes me feel floaty.

Yellow unlike red makes everything around me sparkle.

Black makes me feel heavy, very much unlike red.

Green makes me feel like I'm all wrinkled up. Green is not as pretty as red, pink, or orange.

White makes me feel happy just as I am now.

Purple is the end of the day and my poem.

Eliza Bailey

From *Wishes, Lies, and Dreams: Teaching Children to Write Poetry,* by Kenneth Koch and The Students of P.S. 61 in New York City. Copyright © 1970 by Kenneth Koch. Reprinted by permission of Random House, Inc., International Creative Management and Kenneth Koch.

Feelings

Sometimes you can show how you feel by drawing a picture.

Teacher's Notes

You might ask students to draw pictures that show how *they* feel. After the children have turned in the unsigned drawings, discuss some of them with the class.

28

These pictures were made by children your
age. What feeling does each picture show?

HEALTH AROUND US

Sometimes when you look around, you see things that suddenly make you feel happy.

Have you ever seen a *happy face* like the one shown here? How do you think it makes people feel?

What things could *you* give a happy face?

Teacher's Notes

"Health Around Us" is a recurring feature in this book and in this health series. It focuses on interesting and intriguing aspects of health in the world around us. At times new developments in the field of health will be highlighted.

Here children are asked to think of objects they might give "happy faces." For example, they might transform doorknobs in the classroom into happy faces. Or they might put temporary decorations on their lockers.

Things to Do

Teacher's Notes
Item 3: A "long face" means a sad face, "feeling blue" means feeling sad, "down in the dumps" means feeling low or sad or gloomy, "pig-headed" means stubborn.
Item 5: The hidden feelings are *sad, lonely, bored, scared, nervous, shy, loving, happy, jealous, angry.*
See also page T26.

1. Plan and give a skit in which you are friendly to a newcomer. Later, talk over what friendly actions were shown.

2. Have you recently seen someone who was kind or helpful to another person? Be ready to tell or write about it.

3. Sometimes we use interesting ways to talk about feelings or emotions. Tell what you think is meant by these expressions:

"Joe has a *long face* today."

"Rosa is feeling *blue.*"

"Lou Ann is *down in the dumps.*"

"Stan is being *pig-headed.*"

4. Why are names important to people? What if no one had a name?

5. Look at the puzzle below. See if you can find the names of ten feelings hidden in it.

Write the names of the feelings you find. Be ready to tell why a person might feel each of these ways.

```
Z  B  D  A  N  G  F  S  A  D  X  Y
L  O  N  E  L  Y  B  R  Z  U  Y  E
A  L  N  F  A  Z  W  B  O  R  E  D
O  N  S  C  A  R  E  D  N  V  B  U
E  F  G  N  E  R  V  O  U  S  S  Z
S  H  Y  O  I  U  Y  T  R  E  W  Q
R  X  L  O  V  I  N  G  W  Z  R  T
O  B  V  C  X  H  A  P  P  Y  I  T
J  E  A  L  O  U  S  B  C  W  M  F
S  R  E  N  J  A  B  A  N  G  R  Y
```

Can You Show What You Know?[1]

1. Tell something interesting about yourself that you want others to know. (11–13)

2. Tell three ways in which you are like some others in your group. (14)

3. Act out something a person might do that is likeable (16)

4. Act out something a person might do that annoys others. (16)

5. Explain what you think is meant by "mixed" feelings. (18)

6. Mention two things you can do when you feel shy or scared. (18)

7. Suggest three things a person can do to help get over angry feelings. (20)

8. Suggest something you might do when you are faced with a hard decision. (24)

9. Tell something you might say or do to comfort a friend whose pet has died. (26)

Teacher's Notes

Here behavioral objectives in the *cognitive* area are posed in childlike language directly to the children themselves. In turn, boys and girls give evidence by *observable behavior* of what they have learned.

Other hoped-for behavioral objectives lie chiefly in the less easily observed *affective* area—objectives that pertain to feelings, attitudes, and values. Some of them are:

Is willing to tell others about oneself.

Observes that people are alike in many ways.

Develops some awareness of qualities that make a person likeable.

Practices in daily life what has been learned about shy, scared, and angry feelings.

Grows in ability to make one's own decisions and to withstand group pressure.

Is sensitive to the need to comfort someone who is grieving.

Realizes that a dead pet can still "live on" in one's memories.

[1] Behavioral objectives in the cognitive area are stated here directly to students themselves.

32

Review It

Page numbers show you where to look back in the chapter for information, if you need it.

1. Why might a person sometimes feel like a stranger to himself or herself? (10)

2. What is one good way to become better acquainted with others in your group? (11–13)

3. What are three annoying things that a person might do? (16)

4. What are three likeable things that a person might do? (16)

5. When might a person have "mixed" feelings? (18)

6. What is one time when it is helpful to be scared? (18)

7. Suppose you feel angry because you think a friend treated you unfairly. What might you do to get over your angry feelings? (20)

8. Do you have to do something just because others are doing it? Explain your answer. (24)

9. What can help when a pet dies? (26)

10. What are some things you can do to express your feelings? (27–29)

11. What are some feelings we all have at times? (18, 20, 21)

12. What might help when you are feeling shy about meeting some grown-up visitors to your home? (18)

Health Test for Chapter One

Teacher's Notes
After students have taken the test and their papers have been scored, the test items can serve as guides for a summary discussion. Volunteers can read aloud their rewording of the false statements.
(*Note:* "What Do You Think?" is a special feature that offers pupils a chance to evaluate some of their newly acquired knowledge.)

Copy each number on a piece of paper. After each number write the correct answer, *true* or *false.* Rewrite each false statement to make it true.

T 1. All people have feelings.

T 2. Each person is different from others in many ways.

F 3. Likeable people make fun of others.

F 4. People like it when you say mean things to them.

T 5. Likeable people try to keep their promises.

T 6. Everyone feels scared or shy at times.

F 7. If you feel shy about doing something, don't do it.

T 8. Talking over angry feelings is better than hitting or hurting others.

F 9. You always have to do the same thing others you know are doing.

T 10. All of us want to be liked and to have friends.

Number of Answers   <u> 10 </u>
Number Right   <u>   </u>
Score (Number Right × 10) <u>   </u>

What Do You Think?

What did you learn in this chapter that you think is important? Write your answer on a piece of paper.

SCHOOL & HOME

Teacher's Notes
Special efforts are made in this book and in this health series to foster school-home communication. Here students share with their families ideas about feelings and emotions learned in the chapter. They also try to find out more about their own family members.
(*Note:* Also available from Scott, Foresman to help further school-home communication is the consumable *Activity Booklet* for your class. See page T7 for a description of this booklet.)

You know that it can be fun to learn more about others at school. Now you might try to learn more about your own family members.

Try to find out what kinds of work the grown-ups do. Then when you have a chance, ask your family questions like these:

What did you like to do when you were my age?

Where did you live when you were growing up?

Ask to see pictures of you and others taken at different ages. Looking at family pictures is always fun and full of surprises!

2 Discovering Some Wonders of the Human Body

Suppose someone should ask you, "What is wonderful about the human body?" What would you say?

What are some things you already know about your body? What else would you like to find out?

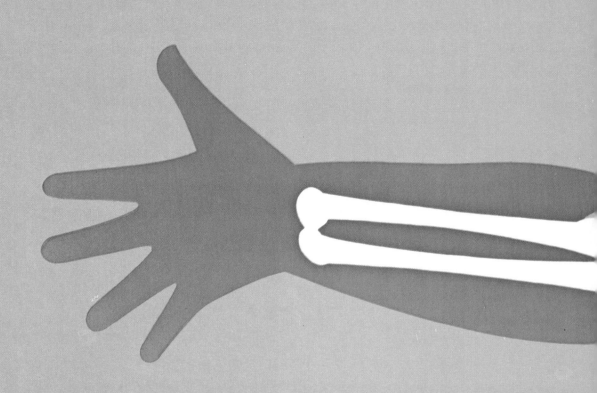

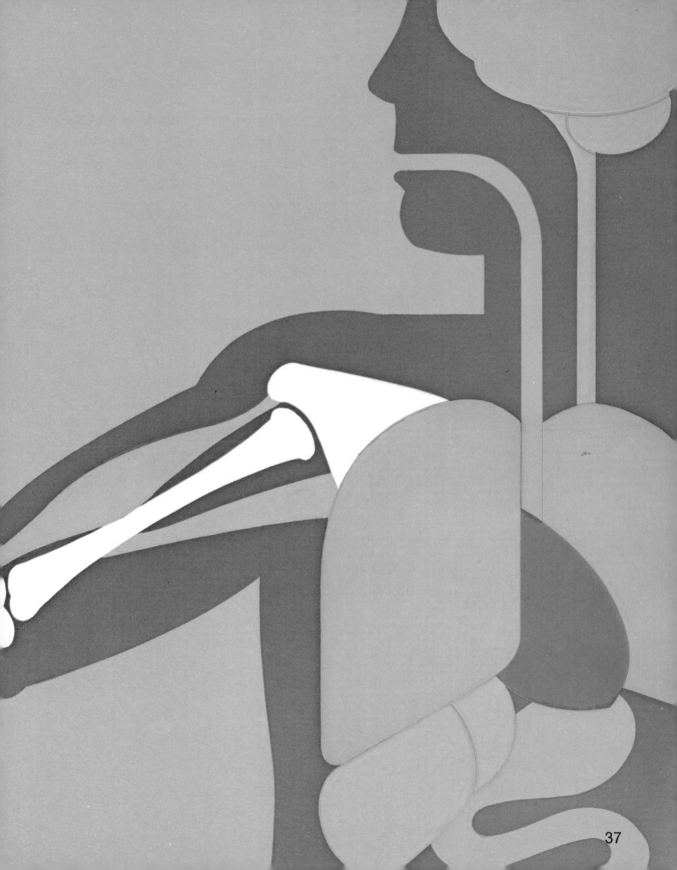

Teacher's Notes
See the Enrichment Suggestions for
Chapter Two on page T27 of the
Teacher's Supplement. See also
suggested Reference Materials on
page T40.
"Preview It" is a special feature that
occurs at the beginning of each
chapter in this book and in this health
series. Here students do some
anticipating. They skim over the main
headings in the chapter. Most of these
headings are, by design, study
questions. Curiosities are aroused, and
pupils are given a framework for the
detailed information to follow.
See also page T27 for additional
teaching suggestions.

Preview It

Take a few minutes to look through this chapter. Find seven questions about the body that the titles ask. Which question interests you the most?

As you study the chapter, try to answer the seven questions. And try to think of your own questions. How might you find answers to *your* questions?

Here is a poem about one wonder you will learn about. Read to find out what it is.

Nobody sees what I can see,
For back of my eyes there is only me.
And nobody knows how my thoughts begin,
For there's only myself inside my skin.
Isn't it strange how everyone owns
Just enough skin to cover his bones?
My father's would be too big to fit—
I'd be wrinkled inside of it.
And my baby brother's is much too small—
It just wouldn't cover me up at all.
But I feel just right in the skin *I* wear,
And there's nobody like me anywhere.

Now look for more information. What else does the skin do besides cover you?

"Just Me" from *Farther Than Far* by Margaret Hillert, Follett Publishing Company. © 1969 by Margaret Hillert. Reprinted by permission of the author.

What Is Wonderful About Your Skin?

The skin is wonderful in many ways. For example, the skin can stretch and fold. And it grows larger as you grow larger.

Your skin also serves as a kind of raincoat. Usually water can't soak through your skin because it is covered with a thin layer of oil. *Oil glands* in the skin send oil to the skin surface. Oil "waterproofs" your skin by keeping water out.

Fingerprints

Perhaps the most unusual thing about your skin is your *fingerprint.* The skin on your fingertips has a pattern of ridges. Look closely and you can see these ridges. You can see the ridges even better with a magnifying glass. This pattern of ridges is your fingerprint.

No other person has fingerprints exactly like yours. How might you make a copy of your own fingerprints?

Skin Color

There is something else that is interesting about the skin. It has coloring matter in it called *pigment.* Pigment helps protect the skin from sunlight. And it gives the skin its color.

There are many shades of skin color. Skin color depends on the amount and kind of pigment in your skin. Except for different amounts of pigment, the skin of every human being is almost exactly the same.

Teacher's Notes

After students read the page, discuss some interesting aspects of the skin. Then you might ask:

"When you bathe, why doesn't the water soak through your skin?"

"In what ways is the skin of every person the same? In what ways may the skin of one person differ somewhat from another's?"

Mention that exposure to the sun causes the pigment in the skin to increase and the skin to darken. This is especially noticeable in light skin. Some people lack pigment in the skin. These people are *albinos.* They have very pale, milky-white skin and very light hair. Their eyes appear pink because the blood vessels give a rosy cast to the colorless irises.

Glossary word: *pigment*

Here are some examples of different kinds of fingerprints.

Teacher's Notes

Discuss the skin's role in helping to control body temperature. Use the drawings on page 41 to help students visualize what happens.
Then ask:
"Where does perspiration come from?" (From sweat glands in the skin. The skin contains about two million sweat glands. More sweat glands are found in the palms of the hands and the soles of the feet than anywhere else.)
"If you were cold-blooded, what would happen when you went outdoors on a very cold day?" (Your body temperature would drop and you would get cold.)
(*Note:* "Sum It Up" is a feature that occurs at intervals throughout each chapter of this book and of others in this health series. Pupils can use this study aid to review important ideas.
Also note that the special features in the margin, such as "Books to Read," are designed to keep children active and interested.)
Glossary word: *blood vessels*
See also page T27.

Control of Body Temperature

Did you know that your skin helps keep your body at about the same temperature?

When the day is hot or you get warm from exercise, you sweat or *perspire.* Drops of sweat come from *sweat glands* in your skin. The sweat moves out of the skin through tiny openings or *pores.* Soon the sweat *evaporates,* or goes off into the air. As it evaporates, your body cools.

There are also tiny tubes or *blood vessels* under your skin. Warm blood flows through them. When you are very warm the blood vessels under your skin get larger. More warm blood comes to the skin surface. Heat from the blood leaves your body and your body begins to cool.

When your body is too cool, the blood vessels under your skin get smaller. Less blood comes to the skin surface. And less heat leaves your blood. Body heat is saved to keep you warm.

Because the human body can stay at the same warm temperature most of the time, human beings are called *warm-blooded.* Most animals, including birds, are warm-blooded. But some animals, such as snakes and frogs, are *cold-blooded.* Their body temperatures become cool when the temperature around them is low.

Sum It Up

What are three or four wonderful things about your skin?

Books to Read

Look in your school or public library for these books:
Elgin, Kathleen. *The Human Body: The Skin* (Watts).
Showers, Paul. *Your Skin and Mine* (T. Y. Crowell).

Inside Your Skin
What do these pictures tell you about how the skin helps control body temperature?

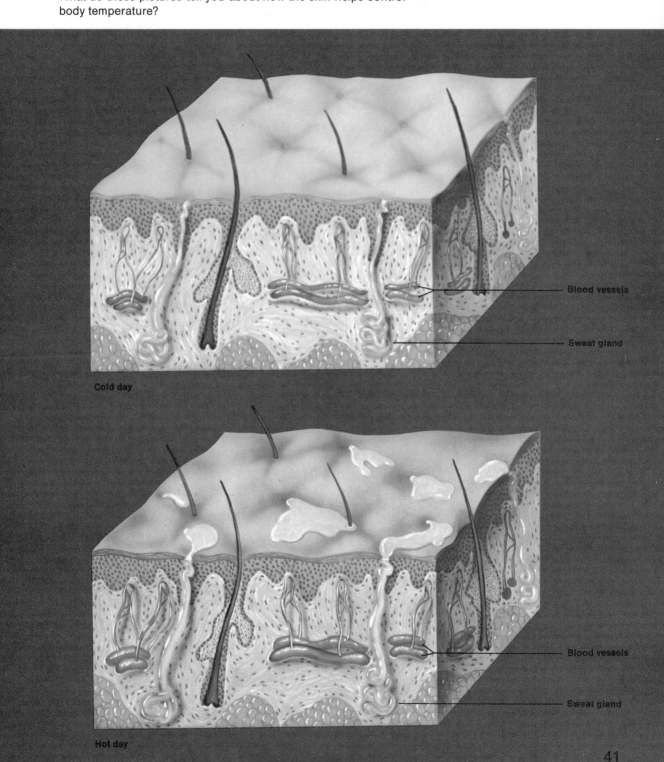

Blood vessels

Sweat gland

Cold day

Blood vessels

Sweat gland

Hot day

What Is Remarkable About Your Heart?

Your *heart* is the amazing organ that keeps blood moving through the blood vessels in your skin. Put your hand close to the left side of your chest. Try to feel your heart beating. The beating is your heart pumping blood to every part of your body.

How the Heart Works

Your heart pumps blood to the *lungs,* back to the heart, out to every part of the body, and back to the heart again. The blood makes each round trip in about a minute.

The blood carries *digested* food and *oxygen* to all parts of your body. The body needs food and oxygen to stay alive and to grow.

The blood also picks up a waste gas called *carbon dioxide.* Your blood carries this waste gas from each part of the body back to the lungs. When you breathe out, you get rid of the carbon dioxide gas.

The Heartbeat

The heart takes a little rest after each pump or beat. But the heart beats every day and night, year after year. It may beat three billion times during your life.

In boys and girls your age, the heart beats about 90 times a minute. A grown-up's heart beats about 70 to 80 times a minute. But the heartbeat is different in the same person at different times. For example, the heartbeat is faster during exercise and when a person is angry, scared, or excited. During sleep, the heartbeat slows down.

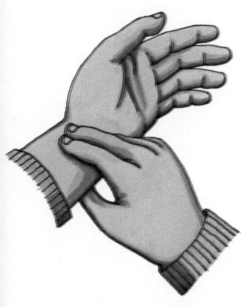

To feel your *pulse,* touch your left wrist below the thumb. Use two fingers from your right hand to do this. Press down gently. Do you feel a push, push, push?

The movement you feel is your pulse. You can tell how fast the heart is beating by feeling your pulse.

42

Exercise and the Heart

When you relax, your heart pumps about two and a half liters of blood a minute through your body. But if you run or jump, your heart speeds up. It may pump as much as seven and a half liters of blood a minute. By speeding up, your heart sends extra oxygen to your muscles. Your muscles need the extra oxygen for energy. But they also produce extra wastes, such as carbon dioxide. The blood carries away these wastes.

When you stop exercising, your heart slows down. Very soon, your heart is again pumping about two and a half liters of blood a minute. Your heart speeds up and slows down when it is necessary. You do not have to think about it. Why do you think this is important?

The Pacemaker

The *pacemaker* is a special bit of muscle and nerves inside your heart. The pacemaker makes your heart beat. It sends signals to the heart muscle. These signals set the speed, or pace, for the beats of your heart.

Many things can change the pacemaker's signals. For example, sometimes messages from the brain can speed up or slow down the signals. What messages might make the pacemaker speed up your heartbeat?

Sum It Up

What is remarkable about the pacemaker?

What are two other wonderful things you know about the heart?

Teacher's Notes

Use the drawings on pages 44 and 45 to help students visualize what happens to the heart when a person is resting and when a person is exercising vigorously.

If students want to listen to the heartbeat, they can make simple stethoscopes out of tubes from paper-towel rolls.

(*Note:* 2½ liters of blood equals about 5 pints; 7½ liters of blood equals about 2 gallons.)

Glossary word: *pacemaker*

See also pages T27–T28.

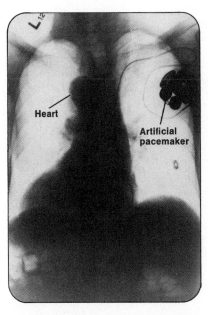

Heart

Artificial pacemaker

Sometimes a person's pacemaker may be slowed down. Then the heart can't pump blood as fast as it is needed by the body.

Medical scientists can put a special kind of pacemaker inside a person's chest. You can see one here. It sends tiny electric shocks to the heart. The shocks make the heart beat the way a natural pacemaker would.

Your Mighty Heart

Here you can see the inside of the heart. Each time your heart beats, blood is forced into blood vessels *(arteries)*.

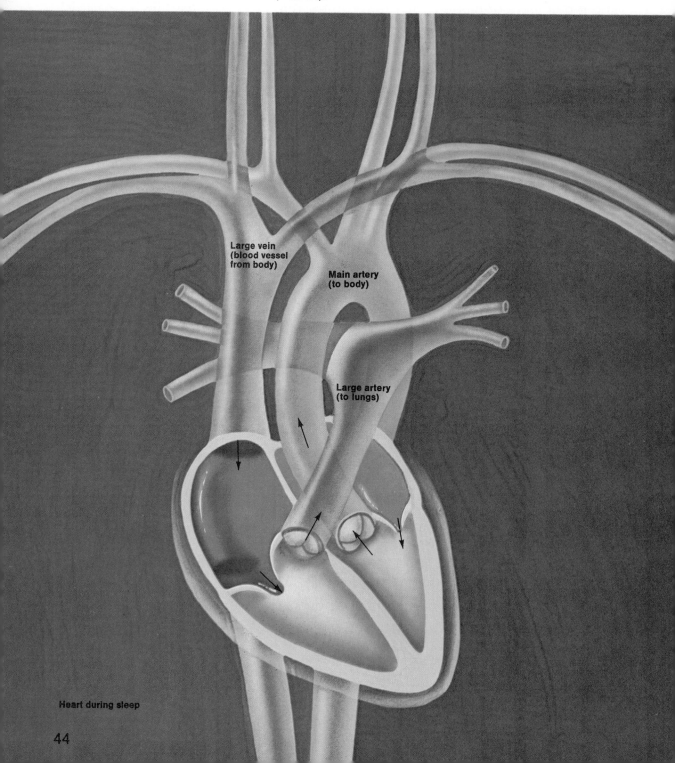

Large vein
(blood vessel
from body)

Main artery
(to body)

Large artery
(to lungs)

Heart during sleep

What Reserve Power Does Your Body Have?

Some of the body's important parts, or *organs,* come in pairs. For example, most people have two eyes, two ears, two lungs, and two kidneys. Now suppose that one of the pair is lost through an accident or an operation. Then the other organ takes over. The organ uses its *reserve power* to do most of the work once done by the pair.

For instance, the kidneys are very important organs. But a person can live with only one kidney. And it is possible to stay alive with half a kidney, if that half is healthy.

If a person's lung is diseased, it may have to be removed. Then the remaining lung will do the work of both lungs. Of course, the person may not be as active as before.

If a person loses an eye, he or she can see with one eye. However, distance, depth, or speed of moving objects may not be judged as well as with both eyes.

A person can also hear with one ear. But he or she may not be able to locate the source of a sound as easily as with two ears.

The body has an amazing ability to make up for many kinds of losses. For instance, a person who is deaf may learn to read lips. And a blind person learns to use his or her other senses to find out about the world. How might a blind person learn to read without using the eyes?

Teacher's Notes
You might mention other examples of the body's reserve power. For example, as much as two-thirds of the stomach can be removed, yet the stomach will eventually stretch to almost its original size and will function effectively. The body can also function without such organs as the gall bladder, spleen, appendix, tonsils, and adenoids.
(*Note:* Many blind people "read" by using a system called *Braille.* Raised dots in different patterns stand for letters. The letters are read by touching the dot patterns with the fingertips.)
Glossary word: *organ*
See also page T28.

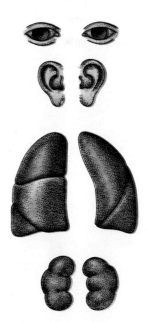

What paired organs do you see here? How does it help to have such organs?

Teacher's Notes
Use the heading to find out what
students may already know about the
body's protective actions.
Ask for a volunteer to demonstrate
how the pupils of the eyes change in
various lights. You might have the
volunteer look out the window or at a
light for a few seconds. Then have
other students observe the size of the
pupils. Now have the volunteer tightly
close his or her eyes for a few seconds.
Again, have others observe the size of
the pupils. Encourage students to try
this demonstration at home, using a
hand mirror to study the size of the
pupils in different lights.
Glossary words: *iris, mucus, pupil*

What Protective Actions Does Your Body Have?

Many protective actions are going on in your body all the time. You do not have to think about these actions. They are *automatic.*

You already know about some of these protective actions. Here are some others.

What Your Eyes Do

If something comes near your eye, you automatically blink. The blinking may keep the object from entering your eye. And if a bit of dirt gets into your eye, tear glands send out tears. The extra tears often wash out the dirt.

Your eyes also control the amount of light that enters them. When you are in a dark place, the *pupils* get larger. The pupil is the opening in the colored part of your eye, or the *iris.* As the pupils get larger, more light enters your eyes. Then you can see better.

When the light is very bright, the pupils become smaller. Less light enters your eyes. How do you think this helps you see better?

What Your Nose Does

Inside your nose are little hairs and a sticky fluid called *mucus.* The tiny hairs and mucus help catch dirt and keep it from going into your lungs. When you sneeze or blow your nose, dust and dirt are carried out.

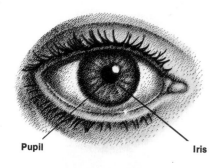

Pupil   **Iris**

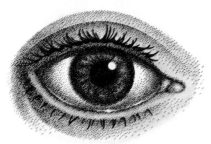

Which eye is receiving more light than the other?

Your nose is also a kind of "heating system." When you breathe in cold air, it passes over a warm moist lining in your nose. The warmed air keeps your body from being chilled.

What Your Ears Do

Inside your ears are wax and some little hairs. They help keep out dirt and insects.

How You Swallow

When you swallow food, it goes down a tube called the *esophagus.* Just before you swallow, a little flap of muscle closes off the opening to your *windpipe.* The flap covers your windpipe so that food can't get into your lungs. If by accident food does enter the windpipe, you usually cough it up right away.

After you swallow the food, it is pushed along by special muscles in the esophagus. The muscles keep the food moving toward your stomach. What do you think would happen if you didn't have these muscles?

Sum It Up

Where is digested food stored in your body?
How does it help to have paired organs?
What are five or six ways that your body helps protect you?

Teacher's Notes
The eyebrows and eyelashes also offer protection. Eyebrows help keep perspiration from running into the eyes. Lashes help screen out specks of dirt before they get into the eyes. After completing this section, you might discuss other protective and automatic actions of the body. Glossary words: *esophagus, windpipe*
See also page T28 for additional teaching suggestions.

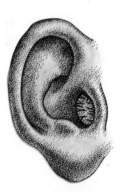
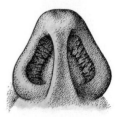

Here you can see the protective hairs of the ears and nose. What is their job?

ENJOY IT

Teacher's Notes
"Enjoy It" pages, such as this one, add richness to students' lives by introducing them to relevant works of art.
Here students can see one of the statues inspired by the strong, graceful bodies of early Greek athletes.
See what pupils know about the modern Olympic Games. Volunteers might seek information and report on details of today's Olympic Games.
See also page T28.

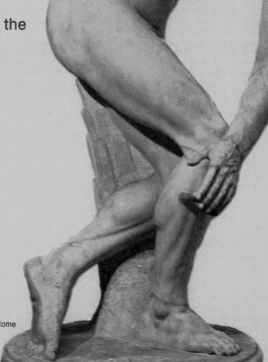

The Olympic Games started long, long ago in Greece. Amateur athletes competed with each other in sports contests.

Sculptors made statues of some of the athletes. The statues were made to show the wonderful bodies of the athletes.

Here you see a discus thrower. The statue was made over two thousand years ago. You can still see a copy of it in Rome, Italy.

What wonderful things about the body does the statue suggest?

Lancillotti Discobulus
Museo delle Terme, Rome

ENJOY IT

Teacher's Notes
Now students have an opportunity to enjoy a poem about the senses. Some effective *group* poems about the senses can be produced by encouraging various individuals to complete statements such as these:
We think these are lovely sights to see. . . .
We think these are pleasant sounds to hear. . . .

A World to Know

Beautiful, wonderful sights to see
And wonderful sounds to hear;
The world is a place for a seeing eye
And a place for a listening ear.

Puppies and lambs and kittens
 to touch!
Satins and silks to feel!
Sugar and salt and honey
 to taste!
Fragrant fruits to peel.

Beautiful, wonderful, pleasant
 world!
And a child who would know
 it well
Has everything to see and hear,
To touch and taste and smell.

 How have your
senses made
life pleasant?

Teacher's Notes
After students complete the page,
discuss what life might be like without
any one of the five main senses.
Suggest that students try looking at
the TV at home for five minutes with
the picture on, but with the sound too
low to hear. Then ask them to try
again with the sound turned up, but
with their eyes blindfolded. Such
simple activities can help children
realize a little of what life would be
like if they could not hear or see.
See also page T28 for additional
teaching suggestions.

How Do Your Senses Help?

How do you know what is going on in the world around you? You have your five main senses to help you. These are the senses of seeing, hearing, tasting, smelling, and touching.

Just think how wonderful it is to have these senses. They help you enjoy your world.

With your eyes you can see pictures. You can read words. You can see flowers and birds, the sun and the moon and the stars. You can see your family and friends. What else can you see?

With your ears you can hear your own voice. You can hear the voices of others. You can hear music that makes you feel happy or sad. What other things do you like to hear?

Think of all the things you can taste with your tongue. Notice that the things you can taste are mostly sweet, sour, salty, or bitter. What are some of these things?

With your nose you can smell good food cooking. You can smell flowers. What do you especially like to smell?

With your sense of touch you can find out if things are hot or cold. What are some other things you can find out?

Your senses also help keep you safe. What are some ways in which these senses help: *seeing, hearing, tasting, touching, smelling?*

What can your senses tell you about each of these objects?

Other Senses

You also have other kinds of senses. Deep inside your body are nerves that tell you of your body's needs.

For example, you have a sense of *hunger* and of *thirst.* These two senses let you know when it is time to eat and drink.

And you have a *muscle* sense that helps you compare the weight of two objects. If you lift two boxes of the same size, your muscle sense tells you which box is heavier than the other. Your muscle sense also helps you control body movements. Your muscle sense helps you walk or ride a bike without looking at your legs. What other movements can you make without looking?

The muscle sense, along with your sense of *direction,* helps you know which way is left and right, up and down, backward and forward.

You have a sense of *balance* too. In your inner ear are some hollow loops that are filled with liquid. The loops are called *semicircular canals.* They help you keep your balance when you walk, stand, or sit.

For example, think about what happens when you twirl around. You shake up the fluid in the semicircular canals. And then you feel dizzy and unsteady.

What do you think are some ways your other senses help keep you safe?

Sum It Up

How do your five main senses help you?
How do your other senses help protect you?

Teacher's Notes
Mention that hunger starts when movements in an empty stomach cause nerve endings in the stomach wall to send messages to the brain. Thirst starts when the lining of the throat and mouth become dry, causing nerve endings to send messages to the brain. The brain interprets these messages as hunger or thirst. (The composition of the blood also affects the brain centers that send messages of hunger and thirst.)
Glossary word: *semicircular canals*

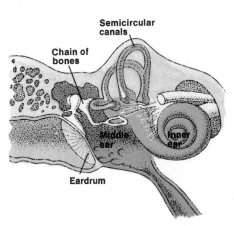

What parts of the ear do you see here? Which part helps you keep your balance?

WRITE IT

What wonders of the human body could you write about? You might write about something you learned in this chapter. Or you might write about something you learned somewhere else. Here is what some children your age wrote.

Teacher's Notes
This chapter on the wonders of the human body is a good motivator for creative writing. Notice the group poem on this page. Often a small group or an entire class can collaborate on such a poem.
See also page T28.

Wonders of the Body

What are some wonders of the body?

A wonder is the heart that beats for 70 years or more.

A wonder is the brain that you use to think with.

A wonder is the skin that makes a waterproof coat.

A wonder is all those blood vessels in every part of you.

Five wonders are the senses of seeing, hearing, touching, tasting, and smelling.

Steve, Julie, Gloria, Lisa, Miguel

What Is Wonderful About Your Brain?

Inside your head is a remarkable organ, the *brain.* You are using your brain to read this book. You use your brain to play games, hear music, and talk to others. And you use it to understand and remember things that are happening around you.

Structure of the Brain

The brain is soft and spongy. It is made up of billions of tiny parts called *cells.* Three coats or *membranes* cover the brain. Between the first and second membranes is a fluid. The third membrane covers the other two. The bones of the head, or *skull,* surround the membranes. The skull, membranes, and fluid protect the brain from falls and blows.

After you were born, your brain grew rapidly. It is almost full size now. But it will continue to grow a little bit each year, until you are about twenty. At full size, your brain will weigh about one kilogram.

Your brain will finally stop growing in size. But the more you use your brain to think, the better it will work.

Structure of the Spinal Cord

The *spinal cord* extends from the base of the brain down the length of the back. The cord contains thousands of *nerves.* It is covered and protected by a chain of bones called the *backbone.* The spinal cord is the expressway that carries messages to and from the brain.

Teacher's Notes
Use the title to initiate discussion about the brain. Such discussion can give you an idea of how much students already know.
Volunteers might seek additional information from reference books and report to the group later.
(*Note:* 1 kilogram equals about 2½ pounds.)
Glossary words: *backbone, brain, cell, membrane, nerve, skull, spinal cord*
See also page T28 for additional teaching suggestions.

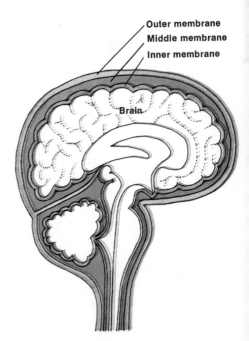

Outer membrane
Middle membrane
Inner membrane

Brain

Three membranes cover the brain and help protect it.
What else helps protect the brain?

Something to Do

You might try to get the brain of a cow or a pig from the butcher. Show the brain to other members of your group at school. Try to find some parts of the brain you read about.

Find out ways to keep your brain working well. Here is a book that might help:

Showers, Paul. *Use Your Brain* (T. Y. Crowell).

How the Brain Works

The brain is sometimes called the busiest communication center in the world. Thousands of messages from all parts of the body are being sent to and from the brain.

Messages are carried to the brain by *sensory nerves.* Special places on the brain receive sensory messages from all parts of the body. For example, messages travel over the sensory nerves from the eyes to the seeing or *vision center.* There are also centers for hearing, touching, tasting, and smelling.

When messages are received by these centers, the brain interprets them. You brain decides what action to take or if any action is needed. For instance, messages leave the *motor center* and travel over *motor nerves* to the muscles. Messages from the motor center tell the muscles when and how to move.

How the Nervous System Works

One part of the *nervous system* takes care of actions you must think about and direct. For example, when you want to talk, run, or play a game, your brain sends messages over motor nerves to the correct body muscles.

Another part of the nervous system takes care of actions you don't think about and direct. Breathing is one action controlled by this part of your nervous system. What are some others?

Sum It Up

How do your brain and nervous system work?

Some Wonders of the Human Body

Suppose you could take off your outer layer of skin. What parts of your body would you see underneath?

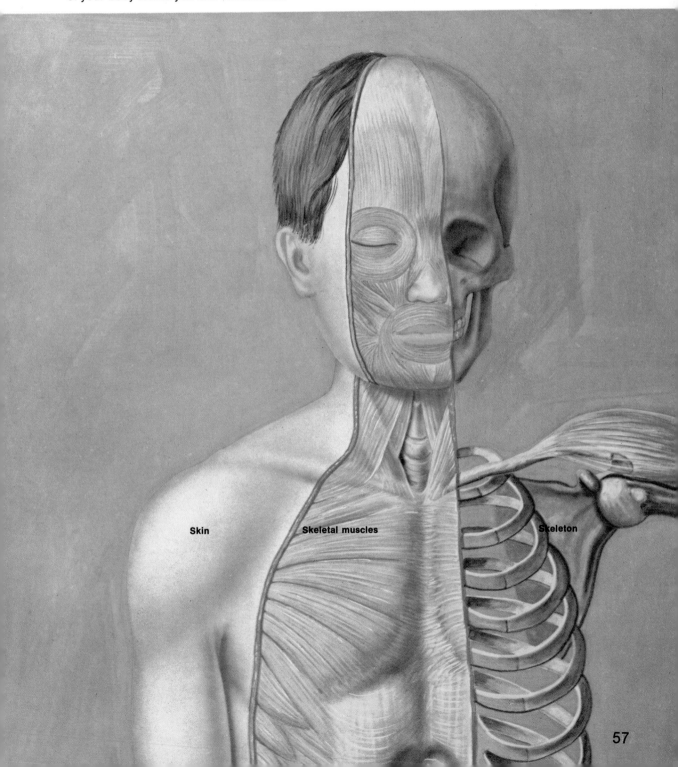

Skin   Skeletal muscles   Skeleton

Some important organs are inside the ribcage you see below.
Why do you think it is important that these organs are *inside*
the bony ribcage?

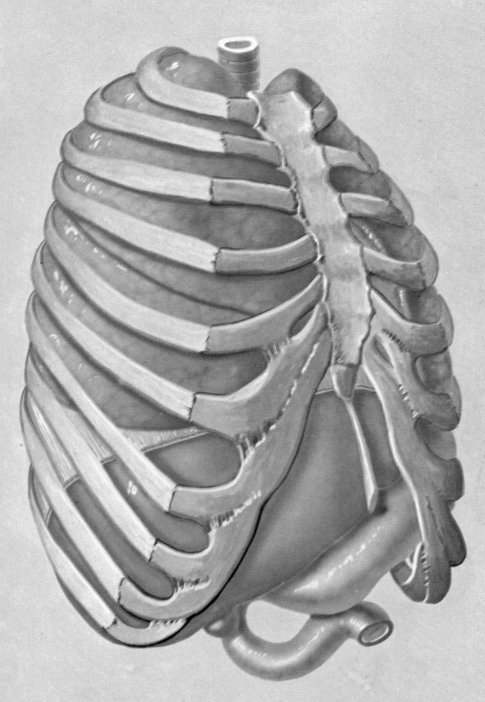

A remarkable thing about the human body is the way that many organs are "packaged" in a small space. What organs do you see here? How are they "packaged"?

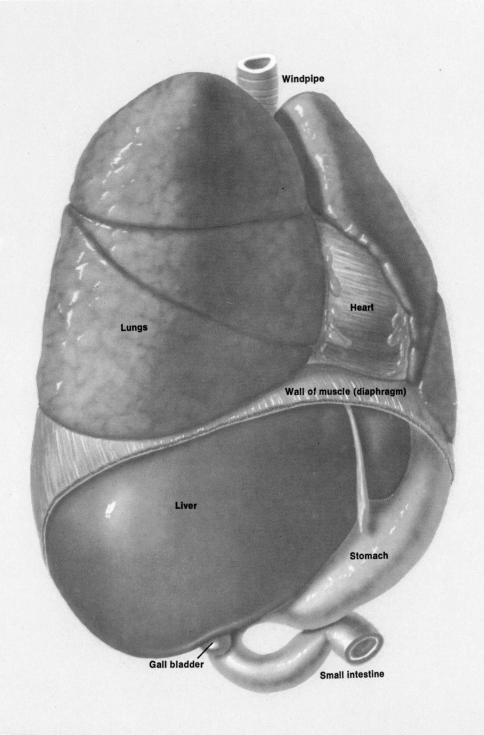

Windpipe

Heart

Lungs

Wall of muscle (diaphragm)

Liver

Stomach

Gall bladder

Small intestine

Blood vessels shown in red *(arteries)* carry blood from the heart to all parts of the body. What do you think the blood vessels shown in blue *(veins)* do?

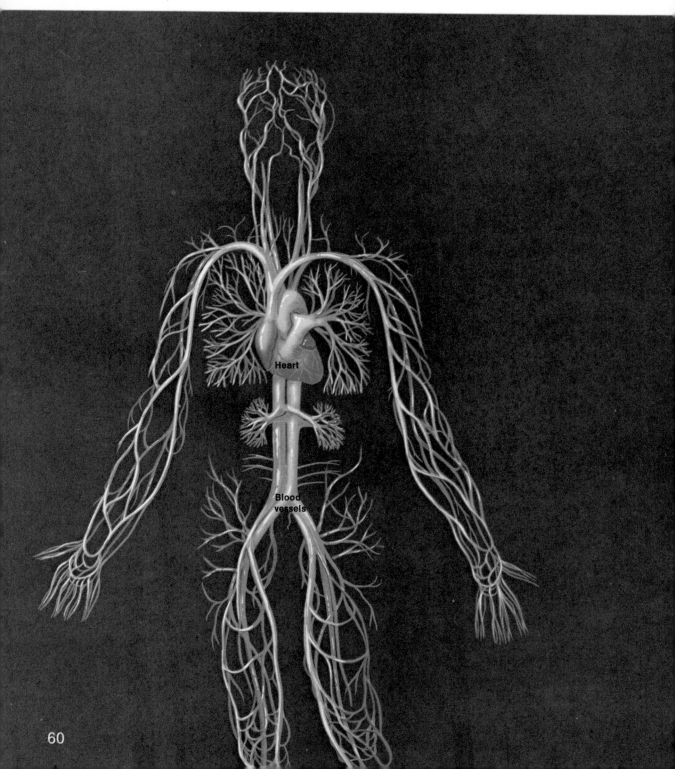

Heart

Blood
vessels

Here you can see the brain, spinal cord, and network of nerves. Some nerves send messages at a speed of 137 meters per second. When would this speed be most helpful?

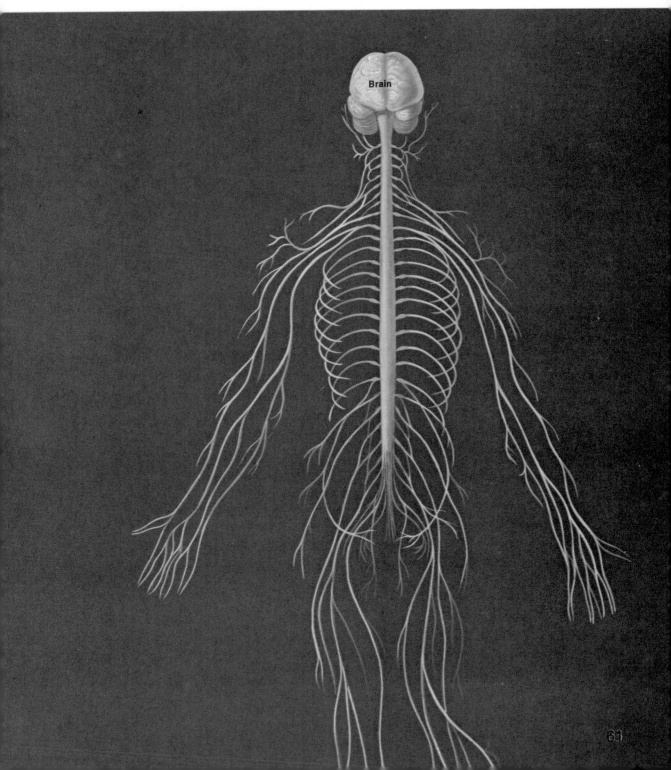

Brain

At birth there were wide gaps in the bones of your skull. By now the bones have grown together and closed the gaps. Why do you think it was important to have these gaps?

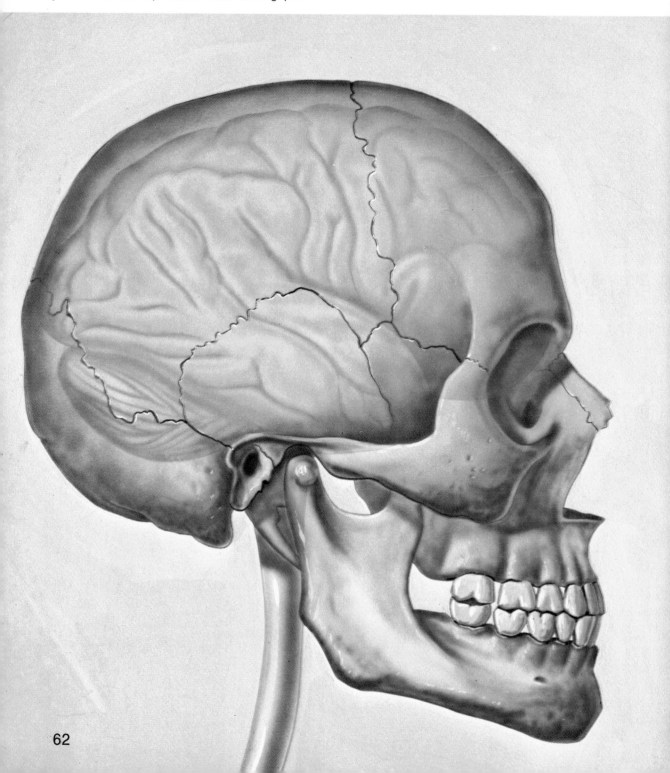

The brain controls your body functions and keeps all parts of
your body working together. What special brain centers do you
see here? What does each of the centers do?

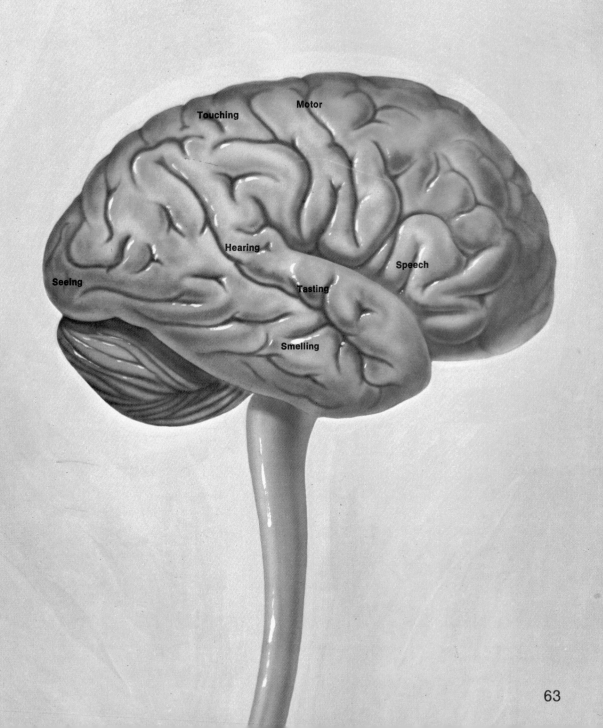

The backbone is made up of many small bones that allow you to bend and twist. The backbone covers your spinal cord. Why do you think your backbone is important?

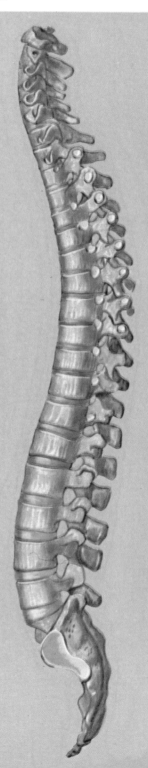

Things to Do

Teacher's Notes
Item 1: The names of the body parts in the puzzle are *brain, heart, skin, nerves, skull.*
See also page T28 for additional teaching suggestions.

1. Find five parts of the human body in the puzzle below. Write the names of the parts you find on a piece of paper. Also write one interesting thing about each part.

```
A R O P B R A I N C Z F
Z X H E A R T O M R O T
S K I N Z R Z Y C F O Y
Z Z F N E R V E S G T P
B B C S K U L L V M X L
```

2. Your heart is about the size of a closed fist. The heart muscles squeeze and relax each time the heart beats.

To get an idea of how strong your heart is, try this: *Make a fist; then open and close your fist again and again.* Your hand soon tires out, but your heart doesn't. Your heart opens and squeezes, opens and squeezes, year after year.

Try to figure out about how many times your heart beats in one hour.

Special Research

Look in the encyclopedia and other books to learn more about the wonders of the human body. See if you can find some interesting facts to share with others.

Here is what one child wrote about.

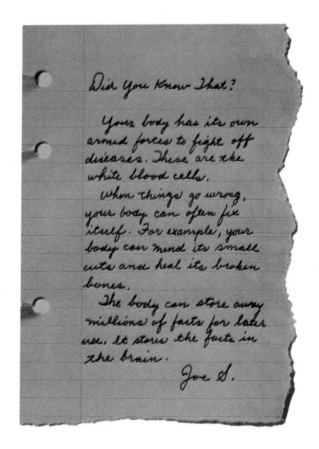

Did You Know That?

Your body has its own armed forces to fight off diseases. These are the white blood cells.

When things go wrong, your body can often fix itself. For example, your body can mend its small cuts and heal its broken bones.

The body can store away millions of facts for later use. It stores the facts in the brain.

Joe S.

Can You Show What You Know?[1]

Page numbers show you where to look back in the chapter for information, if you need it.

1. Explain how the skin helps control body temperature. (40)

2. List two wonderful things about the human heart. (42–43)

3. Explain what the heart's pacemaker does. (43)

4. Explain how the body stores food and water. (46)

5. Explain what is meant by the body's reserve power. (47)

6. Tell about three ways the body protects you. (48–49)

7. Tell what happens when you swallow food. (49)

8. Suggest four ways in which the senses help you. (52–53)

9. Tell one wonderful thing about the human brain. (55–56)

[1] Behavioral objectives in the cognitive area are stated here directly to students themselves.

Review It

Teacher's Notes
"Review It" is a feature that occurs at the end of each chapter in this book and in this health series. It gives children a chance to think over what they have learned, to summarize, and to store away important ideas. Page references after each item make this review page a self-help one. However, group discussion can be a valuable adjunct.

Page numbers show you where to look back in the chapter for information, if you need it.

1. What helps make your skin waterproof? (39)

2. What protects your brain? (55)

3. What happens when food gets into the windpipe? (49)

4. What part of the brain receives sound messages? (56, 63)

5. How does your sense of thirst help you? (53)

6. What is your pulse? (42)

Copy each numbered item from List A. After each item, write the letter and words from List B that best describe it. For example:

7. pupil   g. opening in the iris

List A

7. pupil
8. esophagus
9. iris
10. skull
11. pacemaker
12. sensory nerves
13. mucus

List B

a. tube that leads from the mouth to the stomach
b. sticky fluid in the nose
c. special part of the heart that controls heartbeats
d. bones of the head
e. colored part of the eye
f. nerves that go from the sense organs to the brain
g. opening in the iris

Health Test for Chapter Two

Teacher's Notes
After students have taken the test and their papers have been scored, the test items can serve as guides for a summary discussion. Volunteers can read aloud their rewording of the false statements.
(*Note:* "What Do You Think?" is a special feature that offers pupils a chance to evaluate some of their newly acquired knowledge.)

Copy each number on a piece of paper. After each number write the correct answer, *true* or *false.* Rewrite each false statement to make it true.

F 1. Human beings are cold-blooded.

T 2. Air is warmed as it passes through your nose.

T 3. In a bright light, the pupils of your eyes become smaller.

F 4. You have to remember to breathe.

F 5. Water soaks through the skin into your body.

F 6. Your pulse controls heartbeat.

F 7. All people's fingerprints are exactly alike.

F 8. Sometimes the heart stops beating and rests for an hour or so.

T 9. If a speck of dirt comes near your eyes, you blink automatically.

F 10. When you exercise, your heart slows down.

T 11. Pigment helps protect the skin from sunlight.

F 12. Most unused food leaves the body through the kidneys and urinary bladder.

F 13. The body does not need to store food or water.

T 14. When sweat evaporates, your body is cooled.

T 15. Messages travel to your brain over sensory nerves.

F 16. You have only five senses in the body.

F 17. Food you swallow goes into the lungs.

T 18. Tiny hairs in your nose help clean the air you breathe.

F 19. You think with your skull.

T 20. Your senses help keep you safe.

Number of Answers   20

Number Right   _____

Score (Number Right × 5)   _____

What Do You Think?

Do you think it is worthwhile to learn about the wonders of the human body? Write about your ideas.

SCHOOL & HOME

Teacher's Notes

Special efforts are made in this health program to build school-home communication.

Here students share with their family interesting things they have learned in this chapter about the body.

You might also have volunteers demonstrate what they would do to show a family member how to take the pulse or listen to the heartbeat.

You have learned many interesting things about the human body. You might want to share some of the information with your family.

Is there a poem in this chapter that you would like to copy and read to the family? Which one?

What are some wonders of the human body that you can tell about?

Can you show family members how to feel the pulse?

What could you use at home to listen to the heartbeat? Use the picture below to give you some ideas.

3 Becoming Safety-Minded

Some boys and girls your age think that learning about safety is "just for little kids." What do you think about that idea?

What makes you think that accidents can happen to young people your age? What kinds of accidents do you think happen most often?

What does it mean to become "safety-minded"?

Teacher's Notes
See the Enrichment Suggestions for
Chapter Three on page T29 of the
Teacher's Supplement. See also
suggested Reference Materials on page
T41.
"Preview It" is a special feature that
occurs at the beginning of each chapter
in this book and in this health series.
Here students do some *anticipating.*
They skim over the main headings in
the chapter. Most of these headings
are, by design, study questions.
Curiosities are aroused, and pupils are
given a framework for the detailed
information to follow.
See also page T29.

Preview It

Accidents happen every day. Young people your age have accidents with cars and bicycles. You have falls. Some of you have accidents around water. And others get burns and scalds.

This chapter should help you avoid such accidents. It should help you learn safe things to do. Then you must remember to *do* them.

Look quickly through the chapter. Find five main questions that are asked about safety. Which question makes you most curious? As you study the chapter, keep looking for answers to these five main questions.

Here is a poem about something that often causes accidents. What is it?

J's the jumping Jaywalker,
    A sort of human jeep.
He crosses where the lights are red.
    Before he looks he'll leap!
Then many a wheel
Begins to squeal,
    And many a brake to slam.
He turns your knees to jelly
    And the traffic into jam.

Now begin the chapter. Start by finding out how to keep safe when walking.

How Can You Be a Safe Pedestrian?

Suppose you are walking home at dusk. There is no sidewalk. What safety rules should you always use?

Think about it. Then turn the page and read the ideas given there.

Teacher's Notes

Use the picture and caption to initiate preliminary discussion. Then have pupils compare their ideas about how to be a safe pedestrian with the ones given on page 74.

You might have students check the meaning and pronunciation of the word *pedestrian* in the Glossary.

Pedestrian Safety Rules

When there is no sidewalk, walk on the *left* side of the street or road. Then you can see on-coming cars.

Walk single file on a road with no sidewalks. Why is it important to walk single file?

If you are walking at dusk or at night, wear light-colored clothing or carry a light. Why is this rule important?

When you walk on a street or sidewalk you are called a *pedestrian.* Study the other pedestrian safety rules below. If you follow them, you will not be a *jaywalker.* A jaywalker crosses a street without paying attention to safety rules.

How can each rule help keep you safe?

Obey traffic lights.

At a crossing, look both ways. Look for turning cars. Be sure all cars have stopped. Only then start across the street.

Wait on the curb, not on the street, for turning cars to pass.

Cross only at corners or in crosswalks. Never walk into the street from between parked cars.

Keep alert, even in a crosswalk. Be sure the driver of an oncoming car sees you.

Here is something else to remember. When you plan a walking route, choose the safest one. Choose the one with the most safety aids. What kinds of safety aids should you look for?

Teacher's Notes
Students can discuss the safety ideas suggested here.
Some students might try making up safety couplets. For example, they might finish the second line of these couplets:
When you are walking at night. . . .
At a crosswalk be alert. . . .
Glossary word: *pedestrian*
See also page T29.

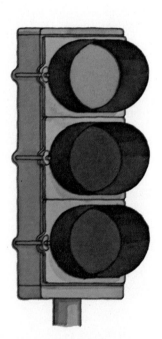

Remember to watch for traffic lights and to obey them!
What should you do when you see *this* traffic light?

74

How Can You Be a Safe Bicycle Driver?

Suppose you are on your bicycle. You come to a crosswalk. Someone is using the crosswalk. What should you do?

Think about this problem. Then look at the rules on the next page.

Teacher's Notes
Use the picture and caption here to initiate preliminary discussion. Then have pupils compare their bicycle-safety ideas with the ones on page 76.

Bicycle Safety Rules

When you drive a bike, you must follow the same rules as a car driver. The car driver stops when someone is in a crosswalk. You must stop too. Here are some other rules for bicycle drivers.

Use the correct hand signals.
Drive single file on streets, roads, or sidewalks.
Stay close to the right side of the street.
Try to drive in a straight line. Don't zigzag.
Drive with just one on a bicycle.
Carry packages in a basket or on a carrier.
Walk your bike across busy crossings.
Slow down as you approach a crossing.
Slow down on wet, slippery, or rough roads.

Also remember to watch for cars that are starting out from a curb or driveway. And watch out for people getting in or out of parked cars.

Do not drive a bicycle that is too big or too small for you.

Never let others dare you to do something foolish while driving a bike.

If you must drive your bike at night, wear light-colored clothing. Have a lamp and clear reflector on the front of your bike. And have a red reflector on the back.

How can each of these rules help keep you or others safe?

Teacher's Notes
Talk over the responsibilities of a bicycle driver. Expand the discussion to include the "why's" of each rule. New safety regulations require wide-angle reflectors on the front and rear of a bike and on pedals, and reflective or retro-reflective material on the sides of tires. If an older bike doesn't have these items, reflectorized material can be placed on fenders, handlebars, pedals, wheel rims, and spokes.

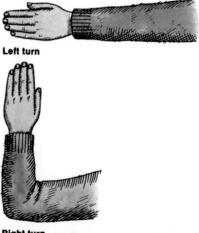

Left turn

Right turn

Stop

Be sure to give correct hand signals when you turn or stop your bike.

What does each of these signals mean?

Some Highway Safety Signs

As a bicycle driver, you must also watch for highway signs. These signs warn you of danger. The shape and color of signs can help tell you what they mean.

What do these signs mean?

Check your answers by turning the page.

Teacher's Notes
Use the highway signs to initiate preliminary discussion. Students will want to check their ideas about shapes and colors of highway signs with those on page 78.

A red eight-sided sign always means *stop*. Don't just slow down. Stop before you enter a crosswalk or intersection.

A sign with a red ball and straight white bar means *do not enter*. You must never drive your bike into a street where this sign is posted.

A sign with a red circle and slash always means NO! In this case, it means *no bicycles.* Don't drive past this sign.

The yellow diamond-shaped sign gives you a warning of danger ahead. These signs always carry important messages. What does this sign tell you?

The round yellow-and-black sign always means *railroad crossing* ahead. Slow down. Listen for the train whistle. Be prepared to stop.

The red-and-white triangle means *yield.* You must slow down or stop, if necessary. Do not enter the intersection until it is safe.

Sum It Up

What pedestrian or bicycle safety rules did you use today?

Adapted from *Illinois Bicycle Rules of the Road.* Compiled by John W. Lewis, Secretary of State. March 1972.

How Can You Help Prevent Falls?

Suppose you are choosing a tree to climb. You want to be sure you don't fall. What kind of tree should you choose?

How can you prevent other kinds of falls?

Turn the page to check the ideas given there.

Teacher's Notes
Use the picture and caption to initiate preliminary discussion. Then have pupils compare their ideas about how to keep safe when climbing to those on page 80.

Choose a tree with low branches and rough bark. And stay out of trees with dead branches. Don't climb a tree with electric wires passing through it. How can these guides help prevent falls?

Remember that most fences are dangerous to climb on. Stay off spiked fences and barbed-wire fences. You should have permission to climb on any fence.

Do not climb on roofs and partly constructed new buildings. Children your age often fall from such places. Your playground may have climbing equipment for you. If so, take turns on it. And stay off the equipment when it is wet.

Many falls happen at home. Look at the items listed below. How could they cause falls at home?

toys on the stairs
spilled liquid on the floor
rickety chair or rocker used as a ladder
failure to use a handrail on the stairs

What other safety guides can you suggest to help prevent falls at home?

Sum It Up

What are some safety guides to remember when climbing trees?

What are some other safety guides you should remember?

What are some things that cause falls at home?

Teacher's Notes

Trees with low branches tend to keep a climber from going too high; rough bark is not slippery and helps prevent falls; dead branches may break off and cause falls; electric wires going through a tree present the danger of an electric shock if the climber touches them. Discuss some consequences of falls—bruises, scratches, broken bones. Also talk over what the words and phrases below suggest about how falls may occur. How might such falls be prevented?

tripping, bumping, pushing,
not watching where you are going

(*Note:* Special features in the margin, such as "Something to Think About," are designed to keep children active, interested, and alert throughout each chapter.)

See also page T29.

Something to Think About

What could cause falls on the playground?

What could cause falls in the school hall?

What could cause falls in the school washroom?

What safety guides can you suggest to help prevent falls in these places?

Dangerous Places to Play
A *quarry* is a place where stone is dug out. Water in a quarry
may be thirty meters deep or more. Why might this be dangerous?

81

Dumps and junkyards are unsafe places to play. Why do you think so? When might old refrigerators and trunks be dangerous?

Parking lots can be dangerous places to play. What are some accidents that might happen to children who play in them?

SECTION
3

Going into empty buildings is against the law and may be dangerous. What dangers might there be in things like broken windows, rotten stairs, and broken railings?

84

It is dangerous to play in or around any kind of place where buildings are being constructed. And it is against the law. What could cause accidents around construction work?

WRITE IT

Burns and scalds are accidents that often happen at home. A *scald* is a burn from steam or a hot liquid.

Here is what some children wrote about things that cause burns and scalds. What can you write?

Can you make a poster and write a safety message to go with it?

Teacher's Notes

You might motivate some children to write about their ideas concerning burns and scalds by using these starters:

One way to prevent a small burn is. . . .

Be careful with pans on the stove. One thing to do is. . . .

Give time for volunteers to read aloud their accounts. Later the writings might be put in a class safety scrapbook.

Stress, if students' writings do not, the need to use potholders, to turn handles on stove pans so people passing by won't bump into them, to test shower or bath water before getting under or into it.

See also page T30 for additional teaching suggestions.

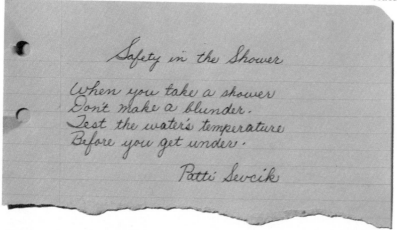

Safety in the Shower

When you take a shower
Don't make a blunder.
Test the water's temperature
Before you get under.

Patti Sevcik

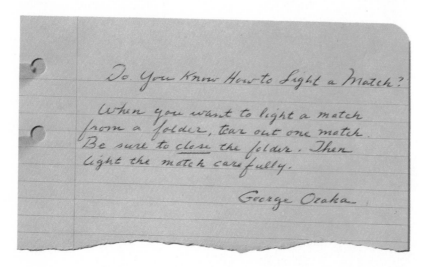

Do You Know How to Light a Match?

When you want to light a match from a folder, tear out one match. Be sure to close the folder. Then light the match carefully.

George Osaka

How Can You Help Someone in the Water?

Suppose you see a child fall into the deep water in a pool. The child doesn't seem to know how to swim. What could you do to help?

Think about what you would do. Then check the answers on the next page.

Teacher's Notes
Use the picture and caption to initiate discussion. Then have pupils check their answers with those on page 88.

Water Safety Guides

If you see someone in trouble in the water, call loudly for help. If possible, send someone nearby for adult help.

Never jump into the water yourself. By jumping in, you risk your own life. And you may not be able to save the other person. Only trained lifeguards should go into the water to help.

What can you do until help comes? If the person is just beyond reach, try extending a towel, a pole, or a tree branch. You can also use an oar or a fishing rod. When the person grabs the object, pull him or her to safety.

If you can't reach the person, throw something that floats. Throw anything that will support the person. You might throw a life jacket, a beach ball, a rubber tire, or a slab of wood.

Suppose you are in a boat and someone falls overboard. What should you do? Again, don't go into the water yourself. Throw the person a life jacket. Or throw anything that floats. Pull the person to the side of the boat. Let the person hang onto the boat and rest. Soon he or she should be able to get into the boat. Remember that each person in a boat should have a life jacket or a "throwable" life preserver. And each person should know how to use it. Why?

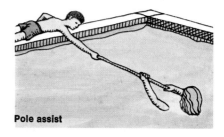

Pole assist

This person is in trouble in the water.

What is the boy doing to help? What other things might you do to help?

Survival Floating

Suppose *you* are in trouble in the water. How can you help yourself?

First of all, keep calm. Don't tire yourself by thrashing around.

Don't try to keep your head completely out of water. If you try to hold your head out of water, you will sink deeper.

Remember that it is easy to keep afloat. The fat and air in your body help you float. And air in your lungs acts like a life preserver.

Next, be sure to use *survival floating.* You can use survival floating for hours, if necessary. The next time you go swimming, practice it. You can see how to do survival floating at the right.

Sum It Up

Tell two ways you could help someone who is in trouble in the water.

What is survival floating?

Teacher's Notes
Emphasize that most drownings are due to panic and to failure to use proper methods for keeping afloat. The majority of drownings occur within a few feet of shore, from a dock or float, or in water of standing depth. Survival floating methods might be pantomimed.
See also page T30 for additional teaching suggestions.

Survival floating

1. Breathe deeply and hold your breath. Put your head down in the water. Relax and let yourself sink.

2. Now paddle slowly with your hands and feet. Lift your head just far enough to breathe out. Take a deep breath and put your head down again.

SAFETY AROUND US

Look at some boxes and bottles of medicine at a drug or food store. What do all the drugs have on the boxes or bottles to help protect people?

See what else you can find out about drugs by studying the picture below.

Teacher's Notes
"Safety Around Us" is a recurring feature in this health series. It focuses on one of the safety problems presented in each of the safety chapters.

Here children are asked to think about some important safety guides for use with *over-the-counter* drugs.

Emphasize that a helpful drug can also be harmful if it is not used in the right way. That is one reason why drugs should only be taken if needed, and why they must be used exactly according to directions.

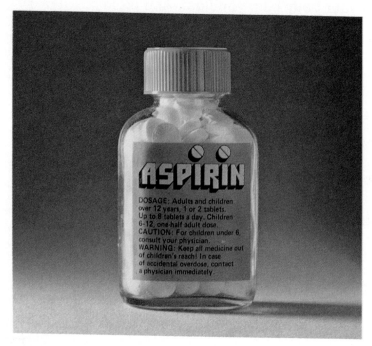

Here you can see the directions on a bottle of aspirin. What information can you find? Why do you think a person should be careful about taking such a drug?

What kind of bottle cap is used on this drug to keep small children safe?

What Should You Know About Drugs?

Suppose someone on TV says that aspirin can help headaches. You have a headache. And you think that maybe you need an aspirin tablet. What should you do?

Turn the page and study the ideas given there.

Teacher's Notes
Use the picture and caption here to initiate preliminary discussion. Then have pupils compare their ideas about drug safety with those given on page 92.

Drug Safety Guides

Don't let a TV or radio commercial fool you. The commercial may make you think that you need a drug. But it is not likely that you do.

Remember, aspirin is a *drug* used as medicine. And taking any drug has some danger. A person can never be sure how the drug will affect him or her. Even doctors do not always know. Thus, a drug may help a headache. But it may have some *side effects*. For example, it might make a person dizzy or very sleepy.

Often you do not need a drug. You may need food or sleep. Or you may need to turn down a noisy TV. But if you really feel sick, tell an adult at home or at school.

You can buy *over-the-counter* drugs *(OTC)* at a food or drug store. Another name for them is *nonprescription* drugs. They are intended for *short-time* use and for *minor* illness. But children should never take any drugs unless supervised by an adult.

A doctor must write a special order for *prescription* drugs *(Rx)*. Then a druggist fills the order. These drugs, like all drugs, must be taken exactly as directed. No one should take another person's prescription drug. Why not?

Sum It Up

What is an over-the-counter drug? What is a prescription drug?

Who should give children any drugs that might be needed?

Teacher's Notes

During discussion of this page, such ideas as these should be stressed:

A drug is something that can make changes in the body. Many drugs are called *medicines*.

Sometimes advertising for over-the-counter drugs exaggerates the need for a drug or creates a problem that does not exist.

Too much of a drug can make a person sick or may even kill the person.

Prescription drugs are generally more powerful than over-the-counter drugs. They must be used with special care.

See if pupils know another word for the druggist who fills prescriptions *(pharmacist)*. A pharmacist is a health worker who has had long and very special training. The pharmacist has a license that permits him or her to fill prescriptions.

Glossary words: *drug, medicine, prescription*

See also page T30.

Something to Think About

What do you think this safety slogan means: *Safety Starts Between the Ears?*

What parts of the body help keep you safe?

Things to Do

Teacher's Notes
"Special Research" offers extra research or investigation activities for advanced students or highly motivated ones. Be sure to provide time later for their reports to be presented to the group. See also page T30 for additional teaching suggestions.

1. Make a safety study of your community. Look for safety aids such as signs, crosswalks, and overpasses. Look, too, for things that could be dangerous, such as quarries and dumps. Later, report to your group about what you have found.

2. Think of some good safety guides to use with each of these things:
   a. a chemistry set
   b. bows and arrows
   c. a baseball bat
   d. skates

3. Watch the headlines in your newspaper. Find some newspaper stories about accidents. Be ready to tell your group how the accidents might have been prevented.

4. Make a safety poster about pedestrian safety. What things could you write on your poster?

5. You can learn how to give *first aid* for minor injuries. First aid is the care given at once to an injury.

Read to find out how to give first aid for bruises and burns without blisters. What should you do?
Bruises

Put ice or cold cloths on the bruise at once. This helps reduce swelling and pain.
Burns without blisters

Run cold water on a minor burn until you feel no more pain.

If the burn is blistered or deep, a doctor should treat it. Do not apply grease or ointments.

Special Research

1. Make a report on what to do in the event of a tornado.

2. Do you think the use of alcoholic drinks might have anything to do with traffic accidents? See what you can find out. Report what you find.

Can You Show What You Know?[1]

Teacher's Notes
Here behavioral objectives in the *cognitive* area are posed in childlike language directly to the children themselves. In turn, boys and girls give evidence by *observable behavior* of what they have learned.
Other hoped-for behavioral objectives lie chiefly in the less easily observed *affective* area—objectives that pertain to feelings, attitudes, and values. Some of them are:

Assumes responsibility for one's own safety.

Practices safety ideas learned in daily life.

Cooperates with school safety rules.

Alerts himself or herself to safety hazards at home and tries to correct them.

Page numbers show you where to look back in the chapter for information, if you need it.

1. List five safety rules for pedestrians. (74)

2. Show these bicycle hand signals: *left turn, right turn,* and *slow down* or *stop.* (76)

3. Write five safety rules for bicycle drivers. (76)

4. Describe three things that might cause falls. (80)

5. Mention five places where it is never safe to play. (81–85)

6. Tell how to help someone who falls overboard from a boat. (88)

7. Explain how to do survival floating. (89)

8. Tell who should give a child any drug that is needed. (92)

9. Explain what an over-the-counter drug is. (92)

10. Explain what a prescription drug is. (92)

11. Suggest an important safety guide in using any drug. (92)

[1] Behavioral objectives in the cognitive area are stated here directly to students themselves.

Review It

Teacher's Notes

"Review It" is a feature that occurs at the end of each chapter in this book and in this health series. It gives children a chance to think over what they have learned, to summarize, and to store away important ideas. Page references after each item make this review page a self-help one. However, group discussion can be a valuable adjunct.

Page numbers show where to look back in the chapter for information, if you need it.

1. Why should you walk on the left side of a street when there is no sidewalk? (74)

2. What is a jaywalker? (74)

3. What should you do if you drive your bike at night? (76)

4. What does a red eight-sided traffic sign always mean? (78)

5. What kinds of accidents do boys and girls your age have? (72)

6. Why shouldn't you jump into deep water to save someone? (88)

7. What can you do to help a swimmer in trouble? (88)

8. What is an OTC drug? (92)

9. What is an Rx drug? (92)

10. What first aid can you give for a bruise? (93)

11. What is first aid for a burn without blisters? (93)

Copy each numbered item from List A. After each item, write the letter and words from List B that best describe it. For example:

12. junkyard   f. dump

List A

12. junkyard
13. pedestrian
14. survival floating
15. jaywalker
16. scald
17. quarry

List B

a. person on foot
b. way to avoid drowning
c. a burn from steam or a hot liquid
d. person who ignores traffic rules
e. place where stone is dug out
f. dump

Health Test for Chapter Three

Teacher's Notes
Volunteers can read aloud their wording of the completion statements and their rewording of the false statements.
All blanks in a completion sentence must be filled correctly in order to score a point for that sentence.
(*Note:* "What Do You Think?" is a special feature that offers pupils a chance to evaluate some of their newly acquired knowledge.)

Part I

Copy each sentence and fill in the missing word or words.

1. Do not climb on the __high__ branches of trees.

2. If there is no sidewalk, walk on the __left__ side of the street.

3. At a crossing, look __both__ ways and look for __turning__ cars.

4. As a bicycle driver, you must obey the same traffic rules as a __car__ driver.

5. Going into __empty__ buildings is dangerous and against the law.

6. A __prescription__ drug is the kind that a doctor orders.

7. Any drug should be used exactly according to __directions__ .

8. A burn caused by a hot liquid or steam is called a __scald__ .

9. A round yellow-and-black safety sign always means __railroad crossing__ .

10. Put __ice__ on a bruise.

11. A __jaywalker__ does not obey traffic rules.

12. Objects left on stairs can cause __falls__ .

Part II

Copy each number on a piece of paper. After each number write the correct answer, *true* or *false*. Rewrite each false statement to make it true.

T 13. It is not safe to play in dumps.

T 14. You should have a light on your bike.

T 15. Parking lots are dangerous places to play.

T 16. Never drive your bike across busy streets.

T 17. All drugs can be dangerous.

T 18. A quarry is an unsafe place to play.

T 19. Never jump into deep water to try to save a swimmer in trouble.

T 20. A grown-up should give you medicine if it is needed.

Number of Answers	__20__
Number Right	_____
Score (Number Right × 5)	_____

What Do You Think?

What did you learn in this chapter that you did not know before? Write your answer on a piece of paper.

SCHOOL & HOME

Teacher's Notes
Special efforts are made in this book and in this health series to foster school-home communication.
This page offers students an opportunity to be "safety detectives" at home.
You might also have a general discussion about how pupils plan to use the safety ideas in the chapter in their daily lives.

Help at home by being a safety detective. Be alert for things that might cause accidents.

Talk over what to do if someone at home gets badly hurt. For example, you might call a doctor or the police. If you don't know how to call, dial zero on the telephone. Ask the operator for help. Be sure to give your name and address.

You might also keep a *safety list* of numbers by the phone. What numbers would you put on the list?

EMERGENCY
Phone Numbers

FIRE	FI 7-1313
POLICE	PO 5-1313
Dr. Ortega	273-1590
POISON CONTROL CENTER	664-7823
Ambulance	337-4681
Janitor	486-8827
MOTHER (work)	486-6938
Father (work)	486-3143

4 Staying Healthy

Here is what one young person said about staying healthy:

"There's not much you can do about it. You either have good health or you don't."

Do you agree? Why or why not?

What would you say if someone asked you how to stay healthy?

99

Preview It

What key words come to mind when you think about staying healthy? Jot down the words on a piece of paper.

Then look quickly through the chapter. What are some things you are going to learn about? Do the main questions in the chapter include any key words you wrote down?

As you study this chapter, look for answers to the questions. You will probably think of other questions too. How might you find answers to your own questions?

Now begin the chapter. Start by reading about foods. Then try to solve this problem:

How can you help fix something that has at least two foods in it from the main food groups?

Start thinking about the problem. What will you have to know before you can solve it?

How Can Foods Help You Stay Healthy?

Your eating habits affect how you feel during the day. For example, what happens if you have no breakfast, or a poor breakfast? You are likely to be tired or cross. And you may be hungry by midmorning. What might also happen to the way you do your schoolwork?

Just eating lots of food won't take care of all your body's needs. Every day you need the right kinds of foods in the right amounts. Otherwise, you won't feel or do your best.

Teacher's Notes
Use the title to start off preliminary discussion.
Youngsters might also act out how a person might look and behave after a day with very little food.

Which meal would make a better breakfast? Why?

Teacher's Notes

Remind students that there are many different meal patterns, and that different families have different preferences. The important thing is the *total day's intake*—and whether it includes enough foods from the main food groups.

(*Note:* "Sum It Up" is a feature that occurs at intervals throughout each chapter of this book and of others in this health series. Pupils can use this study aid to review important ideas.)

Kinds of Foods

No single food can take care of all your body's needs. Different foods do different things for the body.

For example, some foods are better than others in helping make strong muscles. These foods also help you grow in the proper way. Among such foods are lean meats, eggs, dried beans, fish, and poultry (such as chicken).

Foods rich in fat are better than others in giving you energy. Some of these foods are margarine, butter, and nuts. Other energy foods are bread, potatoes, rice, meat, milk, and cheese.

Foods with lots of sugar in them provide "quick energy." Foods like fruit juices, jams, and honey are rich in sugar.

Some foods are better than others in helping keep your bones, teeth, skin, and blood healthy. Among these foods are fruits, vegetables, milk, and cheese.

Water is an important food too. Water and other foods help keep your body working as it should. The different kinds of foods work together to keep you in good health.

You might want to try keeping a food diary. In your diary list all the foods you eat or drink during the day. Put in the amount you eat too. Be sure to include snacks. After several days you can see if you are eating enough of the right kinds of foods.

Sum It Up

Why do you need different kinds of foods?

How can you find out if you are eating enough of the right kinds of foods?

You need different kinds of foods to stay healthy.

How does each of these foods help keep your body working as it should?

102

Keeping a Food Diary

Here is a page from Sue's food diary. You can use it as a guide for your own diary. See if Sue had enough of the right kinds of foods on Monday. Use the food guide on pages 104 and 105 to find out. Did she?

Teacher's Notes
(*Note:* Yes, Sue did get enough of the right foods.)
Notice that the food guide on pages 104 and 105 pictures only *some* of the foods that might have been shown. Emphasize that such guides are only helpers.
See also page T31.

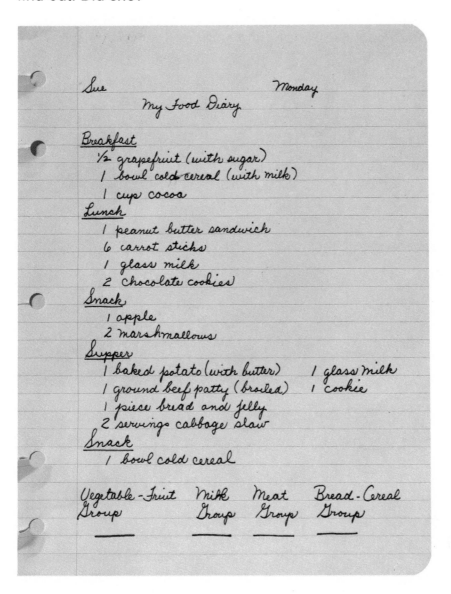

Sue   Monday
        My Food Diary

Breakfast
    ½ grapefruit (with sugar)
    1 bowl cold cereal (with milk)
    1 cup cocoa
Lunch
    1 peanut butter sandwich
    6 carrot sticks
    1 glass milk
    2 chocolate cookies
Snack
    1 apple
    2 marshmallows
Supper
    1 baked potato (with butter)   1 glass milk
    1 ground beef patty (broiled)   1 cookie
    1 piece bread and jelly
    2 servings cabbage slaw
Snack
    1 bowl cold cereal

Vegetable-Fruit   Milk   Meat   Bread-Cereal
Group   Group   Group   Group
_____   _____   _____   _____

A Daily Food Guide[1]

Vegetable-Fruit Group

Four or more servings, including
  A citrus fruit or other fruit or
vegetable important for vitamin C
  A dark-green or deep-yellow
vegetable for vitamin A (at least
every other day)
  Other vegetables and fruits

Milk Group

Some milk for everyone
Children under 9: 2 to 3 cups
Children 9–12: 3 or more cups
Teen-agers: 4 or more cups
Adults: 2 or more cups

[1] Adapted from Leaflet No. 424, U.S. Department of Agriculture.

Meat Group

Two or more servings

   Beef, veal, pork, lamb, poultry, fish, eggs

   As alternates use dry beans, dry peas, nuts, peanuts, peanut butter

Bread-Cereal Group

Four or more servings

   Whole-grain, enriched, or restored

   Add butter, margarine, other fats, oils, and sugar to round out the meal

   Drink at least five or six glasses of water each day

What Foods Can You Fix?

You can help fix food at home that is good for you. The food can also be easy and fun to make. And it may contain more than one thing from the main food groups in it. Can you think of any food like this? What is it?

Here is a food that Pablo often helps make at home. What is it? What things from the four food groups does it contain?

Teacher's Notes
Remind students that they should not light stoves or cook unless an adult supervises. See also page T32.

Now look at page 107. What foods do you see there? How many foods from the main food groups are in each recipe?

You might want to copy the recipes. Maybe you can try them at home someday soon. What other things might you fix that have several foods from the main food groups in them? Who should be there to help you fix them?

Tuna-Cheese Melt

1 small can tuna
¼ cup finely chopped celery
¼ cup finely chopped onion
¼ cup mayonnaise
4 slices tomato and cheese
4 hamburger buns
Mix tuna, celery, onion, and mayonnaise together. Spread tuna mix on each bun. Cover with a slice of tomato and cheese. Bake 15 minutes in 350° oven. Serve hot.

Open-Face Meat-Cheese-Tomato Sandwich

1 slice bread
2 slices canned lunch meat
1 slice cheese
1 slice tomato
1 teaspoon mayonnaise (if desired)
Serves one person

How Can Sleep Help You Stay Healthy?

All day long your brain and your muscles are working. By the end of the day they are tired. Then your brain and your muscles start to relax. Before long, you go to sleep.

As you sleep, the big muscles in your body relax. But they do not relax completely. Your heart also works more slowly. And the muscles that control your lungs work more slowly too. Slowing down gives your heart and your lungs a chance to rest.

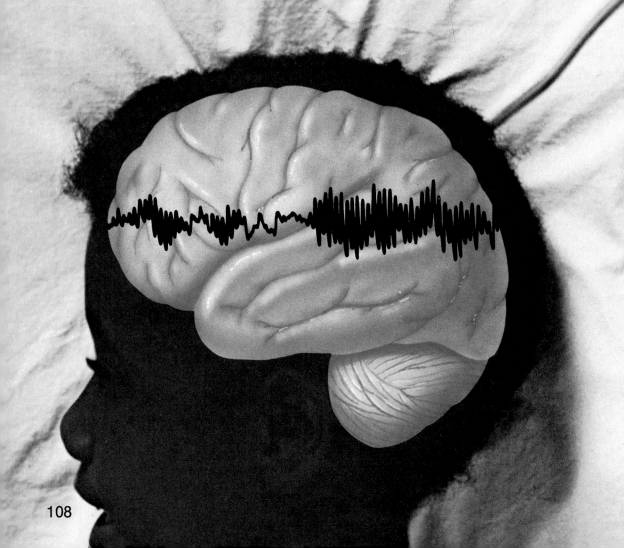

During sleep, some parts of your brain are less active than others. But the brain never stops working completely.

For example, parts of the brain are active when you are dreaming. And part of the brain looks after certain body functions. These functions must go on all the time. Among such functions are the beating of the heart and breathing.

Sleep gives the nerve cells in your nervous system a chance to restore their energy. Sleep helps refresh you. It also keeps you from feeling cross and tired the next day.

Teacher's Notes
If possible, try to get this book from the library:
Showers, Paul. *Sleep Is for Everyone* (T. Y. Crowell). Many good reports can be made by those who read it.

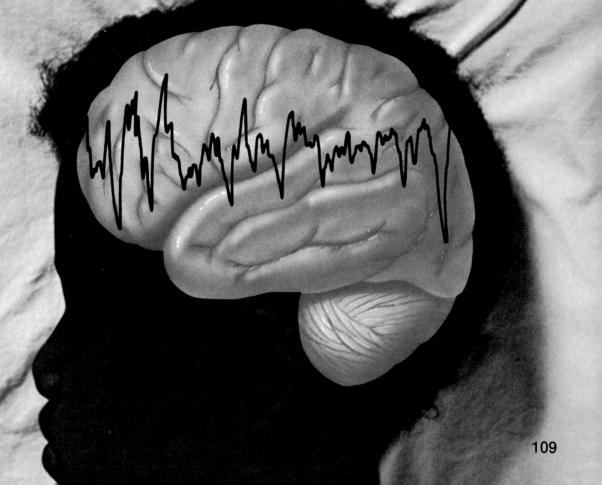

Teacher's Notes
Encourage boys and girls to keep their own sleep diaries for about four or five nights. Volunteers can report their findings later.
Expand the discussion to consider the effects of lack of sleep on posture. Volunteers could demonstrate how a person who is tired and sleepy might move about.
See also page T32 for additional teaching suggestions.

Sleep Needs

Scientists still do not know all about sleep. But they do know that to stay healthy and happy you need to get enough sleep. Sleep also helps you do things without making too many mistakes.

How much sleep do you need? Most boys and girls your age need about eleven hours of sleep each night. But sleep needs differ.

Here is one way to tell if you are getting enough sleep. Notice how you feel in the morning. You may feel sleepy the first hour or so after you get up. This is natural for many people. But suppose you are still sleepy after an hour or so. Then you probably need more sleep.

You might keep a sleep diary for four or five nights. Each night, write the time when you go to bed. The next morning write the time when you get up. Figure out how many hours of sleep you had. Then make some other notes in your diary. For example, were you sleepy all morning? Did you feel cross or tired a good part of the day?

After five days or so, study your diary carefully. How did you feel when you got eleven or more hours of sleep? How did you feel when you got less than eleven hours? About how many hours of sleep seem best for you?

Sum It Up

What are some things that happen in your body during sleep?

What is one way to find out if you are getting enough sleep?

A Book to Read

Suppose you tried never to go to sleep. What do you think would happen? Here is a book that gives an answer:

Showers, Paul. *Sleep Is for Everyone* (T. Y. Crowell). Look for the book at your school or public library.

110

How Can Exercise Help You Stay Healthy?

Exercise is good for you. That is why you often are advised to get plenty of it.

When you exercise each day, your skeletal muscles grow stronger. They begin to feel firmer when you touch them. Your muscles may even become larger.

With regular exercise, your heart also grows stronger. And as you exercise, your lungs take in more air than when you are quiet. Your lungs become able to hold more air. Then you can exercise longer without feeling out of breath.

Exercise can also give you an appetite. How do you feel after you have been playing outdoors for an hour or so?

Games and sports help give you the exercise you need. They are fun as well. And often you make new friends as you play. What game do you know that you might teach to others?

There are also exercises that can help build strong muscles. You might try the exercises on pages 112 and 113. Look at these exercises carefully. Which ones do you think you can do easily? Which might take some practice? When would be a good time to try these exercises?

Sum It Up

What does exercise do for skeletal muscles? What other things can exercise do for you?

Teacher's Notes
Use the title to stimulate initial discussion. Youngsters can then read to find some answers to the questions posed.
You might ask volunteers to demonstrate the exercises on pages 112 and 113. After the demonstration, the exercises can be performed by all the children. Ask students to feel the muscles being stretched during each exercise.
Glossary word: *skeletal muscles*
See pages T19–T20 for a discussion of physical activities and games.
See also page T32 for additional teaching suggestions.

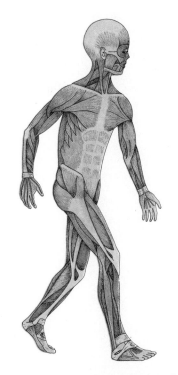

Skeletal muscles are attached to your skeleton. These muscles pull the bones to make you move.

Exercises and Activities for Fitness[1]

Wing Stretcher

Stand erect. Raise elbows to shoulder height.

Close fists; hold them palms down.

Thrust elbows backward and forward rapidly. Keep head erect and elbows at shoulder height.

Repeat 10 times.

Body Bender

Stand with feet apart, arms clasped behind head.

Bend sideward at the hips and to the left. Keep feet in place.

Return to starting position.

Repeat, bending to the right.

Try 5 bends each way.

Deep Breather

Stand erect; feet together, arms at sides.

Lift arms sideward and upward. At the same time, rise on toes and take a slow, deep breath.

Breathe out slowly as you return to starting position.

Repeat 10 times.

Adapted from *Youth Physical Fitness: Suggestions for School Programs.* President's Council on Physical Fitness and Sports, 1973.

Jumping Jack

Stand at attention, with feet together and arms at sides.

Swing arms sideward and upward. At the same time, jump and push feet sideward and apart.

Spring back to starting position.

Repeat 10 times.

Windmill

Stand with feet apart and knees straight. Extend arms sideward to shoulder level.

Twist and bend trunk. Touch right hand to left toe.

Return to starting position.

Now touch left hand to right toe.

Repeat 10 times.

Jog in Place

Jog slowly in place.

Then jog twice as fast.

Lift the knees high. Pump the arms vigorously.

Then slow down to an easy jog again.

Jog 25 times slowly, 25 times fast, and 25 times slowly.

ENJOY IT

Paul Klee's picture has been called one that *moves*. What do you think of this description? How would you make a picture that moves?

Teacher's Notes

This really is a picture to enjoy! See if youngsters can discover the girl's playmate (a goose). Also ask what is interesting about the girl's eyes. (One is a ball to play with; the other is an "s" to see with.)
See also page T32 for additional teaching suggestions.

A Child's Game
Paul Klee
S.P.A. D.E.M., Paris

HEALTH AROUND US

In many places you see signs like the one below. What does the sign say? Do you think the sign is posted to help people stay healthy?

Teacher's Notes
"Health Around Us" is a recurring feature in this book and in this health series. On this page children discover what the community does to help discourage smoking (a health hazard). Invite pupils to look around them in the next few days for No Smoking signs. Take time later for their reports. Glossary words: *cancer, emphysema* See also page T32.

NO SMOKING

FAVOR DE NO FUMAR

DÉFENSE DE FUMER

You may know that cigarette smoking can cause lung *cancer.* It can also cause *emphysema,* another disease of the lungs. Smoking can lead to problems with the heart and blood vessels too.

There is another reason for the sign above. People who are near smokers may be annoyed by the smoke. The smoke may make nonsmokers cough or sneeze. And it may make their eyes water or burn.

Why do you think No Smoking signs are important to people's health?

How Do You and Others Grow in Healthy Ways?

Each boy or girl grows in his or her own way. Each has his or her own timetable for growing. Some boys and girls your age may not be growing much now. Others may be starting to "shoot up" and to gain weight.

Body Builds

Young people differ in body builds. Some children are short and thin. Some are short and stocky. Some are tall and stocky. Others are tall and thin. Differences in body builds are to be expected. Each person is different from others in many ways.

When you think about differences in weight, keep body builds in mind. Thus, a tall, stocky boy or girl is apt to weigh more than a tall, thin one. And a short, thin boy or girl will usually weigh less than a short, stocky one. You must expect great differences in weight among boys and girls your age.

Growth Patterns

Healthy nine- and ten-year-old girls range widely in size. Such differences are usual for girls this age. Nine- and ten-year-old boys also vary widely in size. Yet all these boys are growing as they should.

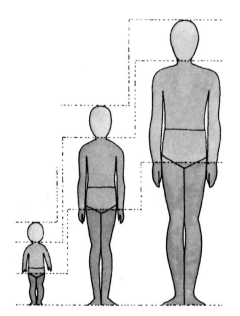

Your head doubles in size from the time you are a baby until the time you are fully grown.

Your trunk grows three times its original size.

Your legs grow in length almost five times their original size.

Around the age of nine or ten, some girls start growing taller. They make greater gains in height than boys their age do. Many girls between the ages of nine and thirteen are taller than boys their age. But around the age of thirteen, most boys begin to "catch up." They grow taller than many girls their age.

Remember that some boys and girls are fairly tall or short at *all* ages. Some young people grow up faster, and some more slowly than others.

Usually, if you follow the guides for healthful living, you will grow as you should. These health guides include getting enough of the right foods, but not too much. Other guides are getting enough sleep, rest, and exercise.

Now turn to the charts on pages 118–121. What can you find out about how your body changes as you grow?

Sum It Up

Why might a friend your age be very different in size from you?

What health guides can you follow to help you grow as you should?

At what ages might you find many girls taller than many boys the same age?

Teacher's Notes
Discuss what young people can do to help themselves grow in the way that is right for them.
Also point out that good health practices—such as getting a proper diet, and getting enough sleep and exercise—contribute to good posture. Take time to discuss in detail the general growth patterns pictured on pages 118-121.
See also page T32 for additional teaching suggestions.

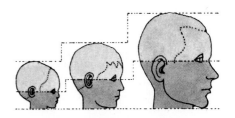

Notice how the head changes from babyhood to adulthood.

Some Ways That Boys and Girls Grow

How would you use the pictures on this page and the next to explain individual differences in growing?

Nine-year-old girls
Height range: 122 to 135 centimeters
Weight range: 22 to 41 kilograms

Ten-year-old girls
Height range: 127 to 152 centimeters
Weight range: 23 to 45 kilograms

Nine-year-old boys
Height range: 124 to 147 centimeters
Weight range: 23 to 41 kilograms

Ten-year-old boys
Height range: 129 to 152 centimeters
Weight range: 25 to 50 kilograms

Here you can see and read about some general growth patterns
for boys and girls from age five to seventeen or so. What can
you learn about how boys and girls tend to grow up?

At five years of age, boys and girls are usually about the same height.

From five to nine or ten, the boys may be a little taller than the girls their age.

Around eleven or so, there may be a number of girls who are taller than the boys in their class.

At thirteen or so, boys are usually taller. After this age, girls grow some, but not a lot. Boys keep growing until seventeen or older.

Maybe your group would like to make a magazine. In it you could put things you have learned about staying healthy.

Here is part of a magazine one group made. What can you learn from the magazine? What do you like best? What would you like to try?

OUR HEALTH MAGAZINE

Keep Healthy

Make yourself go to bed on time.

Eat enough foods of the right kind.

Get enough exercise.

Meg Calanni

What a Cup of Milk Would Say If it could talk

What's wrong with coffee and tea?
Just one thing you see.
If you always drink THEM,
you may not drink ME!

Amy Levi

Don't Let Foods Spoil

Germs grow very slowly in cold places. So keep foods like milk, eggs, butter, meat, and fish in the refrigerator. If you want to stop germs in foods from growing at all, FREEZE them.

Alan

Who?

Who grows just like you?

N B DY

Ken Chung

What could *you* write for a health magazine? Could you make up a riddle about how a doctor or the school nurse helps?

Could you make a scrambled-letter puzzle about one thing that keeps you healthy? Could you tell about a book you have read and liked?

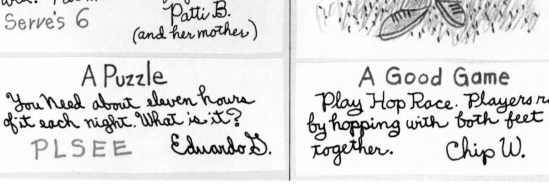

Peanut Butter Milk

1½ Cups nonfat dry milk

2 tablespoons sugar

⅓ cup peanut butter (in a large bowl)

Add dry milk and sugar to the water. Beat until smooth. Add milk slowly to the peanut butter. Mix well. Put in the refrigerator.

Serve's 6

Patti B.
(and her mother)

My Favorite Sport

A Puzzle

You need about eleven hours of it each night. What is it?

PLSEE   Eduardo D.

A Good Game

Play Hop Race. Players race by hopping with both feet together.

Chip W.

Can You Show What You Know?[1]

Page numbers show you where to look back in the chapter for information, if you need it.

1. Tell three ways in which foods can help you. (102)

2. List four main food groups. Tell how much you need daily from each group. (104–105)

3. Explain why part of the brain must be active during sleep. (109)

4. Give two reasons why you need sleep. (110)

5. Tell about how many hours of sleep young people your age need each night. (110)

6. List three things exercise can do for you. (111)

7. Demonstrate one good exercise. (112–113)

8. Tell how cigarette smoking can harm people's health. (115)

[1] Behavioral objectives in the cognitive area are stated here directly to students themselves.

Review It

Teacher's Notes
"Review It" is a feature that occurs at the end of each chapter in this book and in this health series. It gives children a chance to think over what they have learned, to summarize, and to store away important ideas. Page references after each item make this review page a self-help one. However, group discussion can be a valuable adjunct.

Page numbers show you where to look back in the chapter for information, if you need it.

1. Why do you need to eat different kinds of foods? (102)

2. How can exercise change your muscles? (111)

3. What might give a clue that you have not had enough sleep? (110)

4. What are some things that have more than one food from the main food groups in them? (106–107)

5. What might you say to someone who is worried because he or she is not growing as tall as a friend of the same age? (116–117)

6. Which parts of the body may be harmed by cigarette smoking? (115)

blood vessels	knees
ears	lungs
hair	wrists
heart	

7. Use the food guide on pages 104–105 to check the day's menu shown below. Are enough of the right kinds of foods included for the day?

Breakfast
½ serving
   buttered grits
1 glass milk
1 tangerine

Lunch
1 fried egg
   sandwich
2 cookies
1 glass milk

Supper
1 large bowl
   bean soup
2 pieces
   cornbread
2 servings turnip
   greens
1 serving canned
   peaches

Snacks
½ peanut-butter-
   and-jelly
   sandwich
1 glass milk

Health Test for Chapter Four

Teacher's Notes
After students have taken the test and their papers have been scored, the test items can serve as guides for a summary discussion. Volunteers can read aloud their rewording of the false statements.
(*Note:* "What Do You Think?" is a special feature that offers pupils a chance to evaluate some of their newly acquired knowledge.)

Copy each number on a piece of paper. After each number write the correct answer, *true* or *false.* Rewrite each false statement to make it true.

F 1. You need just one kind of food to take care of all your body's needs.

F 2. Foods rich in fat give you "quick energy."

T 3. Exercise can help your heart grow stronger.

T 4. Water helps keep your body working as it should.

F 5. A very useful food guide is this: "Eat lots and lots of food daily."

T 6. Some foods give you more energy than others.

T 7. During sleep some parts of your brain stay active.

T 8. Sleep helps refresh you.

F 9. You need about 7 hours of sleep each night.

T 10. People who are near smokers may start to cough or sneeze from the smoke.

F 11. All nine-year-old girls should weigh the same.

12. People have different body builds.

F 13. All children the same age grow in the same way.

T 14. Exercise can help build strong muscles.

T 15. Smoking is harmful to health.

T 16. During sleep, your heart and lungs slow down somewhat.

T 17. Smoke from a cigarette may annoy someone nearby.

T 18. Lack of sleep can make you tired and cross.

T 19. Some boys and girls are fairly tall or short at all ages.

F 20. Everyone needs exactly the same amount of sleep.

Number of Answers	20
Number Right	_____
Score (Number Right × 5)	_____

What Do You Think?

What is one important thing you learned in this chapter? Why is it important to your health? Write your answer on a piece of paper.

SCHOOL & HOME

Teacher's Notes
Special efforts are made in this book and in this health series to foster school-home communication. Children are usually intrigued by the idea of writing health contracts, such as the ones on this page. However, no pressure should be put on any child to prepare such a contract. For those who decide to write contracts, encourage them to start off with just *one* item.

One group of children made health *contracts* with their families. A contract is an agreement. Here are some health contracts the children made:

"I will try to get exercise by walking when I can. I won't always ask for rides."

"On school nights I'll try to go to bed on time."

What contract might you make? (Don't make one unless you think you are willing and able to keep it.)

5 Learning About Teeth

Do you think there are many children who have no cavities? Why do you think as you do?

What do you think of this statement: "Everybody needs to know how to take care of the teeth"?

What are some things you want to learn about your teeth and their care?

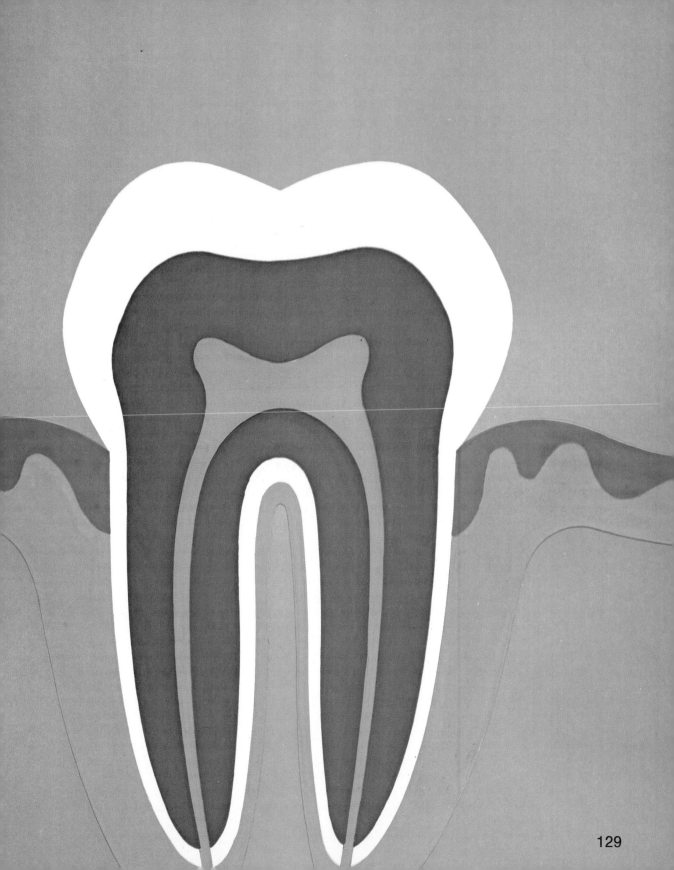

129

Teacher's Notes
See the Enrichment Suggestions for
Chapter Five on page T33 of the
Teacher's Supplement. See also
suggested Reference Materials on page
T43.
"Preview It" is a special feature that
occurs at the beginning of each chapter
in this book and in this health series.
Here students do some *anticipating*.
They skim over the main headings in
the chapter. Most of these headings
are, by design, study questions.
Curiosities are aroused, and pupils are
given a framework for the detailed
information to follow.
The riddles are included to give added
interest and a touch of fun. (Answers
are on pages 132, 137, and 138.)
See also page T33 for additional
teaching suggestions.

Preview It

Almost everyone in this country has some tooth cavities. So it is important that people learn about teeth and their care. With proper care of the teeth, many cavities can be prevented.

Look quickly through this chapter. Can you find four main questions asked about the teeth? Which question makes you most curious?

As you study this chapter, keep looking for answers to the main questions. Think of some questions of your own too. How will you find answers to your questions?

You can have some fun as you read this chapter. You can find answers to riddles about the teeth. Here are some "just-for-fun" riddles.

Riddle 1: *How are a tooth and a king alike?*

Riddle 2: *In what way are teeth like trains?*

Riddle 3: *What two letters of the alphabet name a dental health problem?*

Can you answer any of the riddles now?

Keep on the lookout for answers as you read the chapter.

Why Do You Need Your Teeth?

Every tooth has its special work to do. And every tooth is needed.

Teeth in your upper and lower jaws work together to cut, tear, and grind your food. Food begins to be digested in the mouth when it is chewed and mixed with saliva. And if even a few teeth are missing, you cannot chew properly.

There are some other reasons why you need your teeth. You need them to help you speak clearly. You need them to help you pronounce words with the letters *f, g, j,* and *s* in them. Try saying these words: *fifty, gum, jelly, scissors.* What do your teeth do as you say these words?

You also need your teeth to help give your face its proper shape. If too many permanent teeth are lost, the shape of the lower part of the face may change.

Teeth help you look attractive too. A smile improves the way anyone looks. When your smile shows clean, well-cared-for teeth, your appearance is even better. A cigarette smoker's teeth may not look attractive, though. Do you know why this might be?

Sum It Up

What do you think it would be like if you had no teeth?

List four reasons why you need your teeth.

Teacher's Notes
Use the question posed in the title to stimulate initial discussion. After students have studied the page you might ask:
"What are the advantages of having a full set of teeth in the mouth?"
"Why do you think people generally try to keep their own teeth rather than have false teeth or dentures?"
(*Note:* The "Sum It Up" feature appears at intervals throughout each chapter of this book and of others in the health series. Pupils can use this study aid to review important ideas.)
See also page T33.

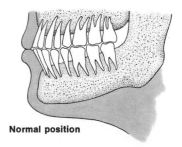

Normal position

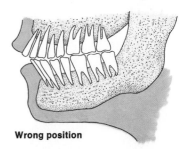

Wrong position

Sometimes teeth grow into the wrong position.

What kinds of problems might be caused by teeth that are out of place?

Teacher's Notes
Use the question in the title to pique
student interest. Then have students
read to find out what information this
page supplies on the makeup of the
teeth. As they read, students might
refer to the diagram on page 133 to
find the *enamel, cementum, dentin,
pulp,* and *periodontal membrane.* You
might also have them consult a
dictionary for the pronunciation of
Glossary words listed below.
Discuss how blood vessels and nerves
get into the teeth. Explain that blood
brings digested food and oxygen to
the cells of the teeth and carries away
wastes.
Glossary words: *cementum, crown,
dentin, enamel, gum, periodontal
membrane, pulp, root*
See also page T33 for additional
teaching suggestions.

What Are Teeth Made Of?

The part of the tooth that you can see is the *crown.* You chew with the crown. *(Now you know the answer to Riddle 1. Both a tooth and a king have a crown!)*

The *root* is the part of the tooth under the *gums.* Some teeth have one long root. Others have two, three, or four roots. You can see the crown and the root at the left.

The crown has a white covering called *enamel.* Enamel is very hard. It is even harder than your bones. Enamel protects the tooth from injury. And it helps keep out germs that cause tooth cavities. If the enamel is injured, it does not come back. It is gone forever.

The root of the tooth is covered by a bonelike material called *cementum.* Elasticlike fibers attach the root firmly to the jawbone. These fibers are the *periodontal membrane.*

Inside the enamel and cementum is the *dentin.* Dentin is also a hard, bonelike material. But it is not as hard as enamel. Dentin makes up the largest part of the tooth. When a cavity spreads into dentin, it may cause a toothache.

The center of the tooth is filled with soft material called *pulp.* Blood vessels and nerves are in the pulp. They enter through an opening in the root. If you have a bad toothache, the pulp may well be the part that aches.

Can you find the different parts of the tooth on the opposite page? What are they?

Sum It Up

How would you explain these terms: *enamel, cementum, dentin, pulp?*

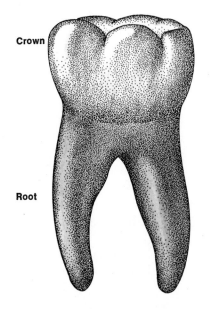

Crown

Root

132

The Inside of a Tooth

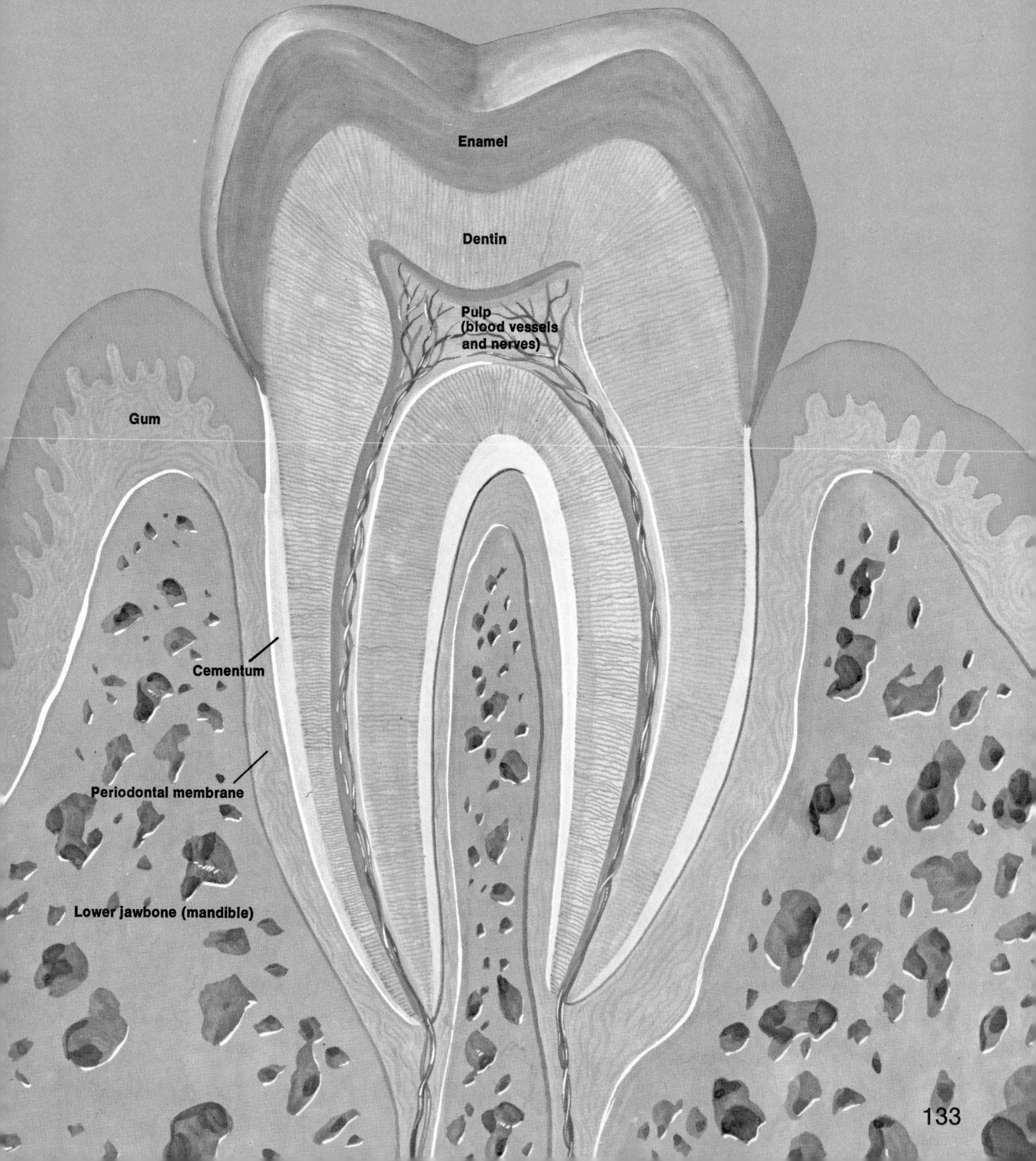

Enamel

Dentin

Pulp
(blood vessels
and nerves)

Gum

Cementum

Periodontal membrane

Lower jawbone (mandible)

Why Are Different-Shaped Teeth Useful?

Have you ever looked at some of your teeth that have come out? Or have you seen a model of all the teeth? If so, you know that teeth have different shapes. Teeth in the upper jaw are matched by ones of the same shape in the lower jaw.

Teeth of different shapes do different jobs. But all the teeth work together to break up and to chew food.

Incisors and Cuspids

The front teeth in your mouth are *incisors.* You have eight incisors. There are four in the upper jaw and four in the lower jaw. The incisors have straight, sharp edges. They cut food, much as a pair of scissors would. For example, suppose you eat an apple or a piece of celery. The incisors are used to bite off the pieces.

Then the pieces of food are moved to the sides of the mouth. The *cuspids* go to work next. Cuspids are the teeth next to the incisors. You have four cuspids. And each cuspid has one point or *cusp.* The sharp points of the cuspids tear apart coarse foods.

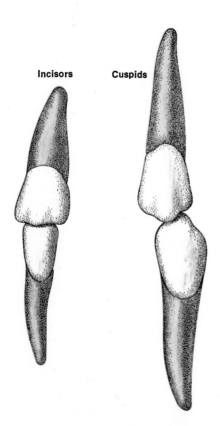

Incisors   **Cuspids**

Bicuspids and Molars

Next to the cuspids are the *primary molars.* But sometime between age ten and eleven you lose the primary molars. Teeth called *bicuspids* grow in to replace them. You will have eight bicuspids when all your permanent teeth come in.

The bicuspids have two points or cusps. These cusps are used to break up and crush food into small bits.

Finally, you really begin to chew the food. You do this chewing with the *molars.* The molars are in the back of your mouth. They have broad tops with four or five cusps. The molars are used to grind food into very tiny bits.

You will have twelve molars when all your permanent teeth come in. There will be three molars on each side of the upper jaw. And there will be three on each side of the lower jaw. You will be about age seventeen when the last molars start to come in. These last molars are called the third molars or *wisdom teeth.*

Sum It Up

What four different kinds of teeth do you have? What does each kind of tooth do?

Teacher's Notes

After study of the page you might ask: "What are bicuspids? Molars?"

"Do you have any bicuspids in your mouth as yet? Are they in your upper or lower jaw?" (If hand mirrors are available, students can profit from using them to study the teeth in their mouths.)

"What will be the last teeth to come through in your mouth?" (Some people never do get any wisdom teeth. They are present below the gum, but do not erupt.)

Glossary words: *bicuspid, molar*

See also page T34 for additional teaching suggestions.

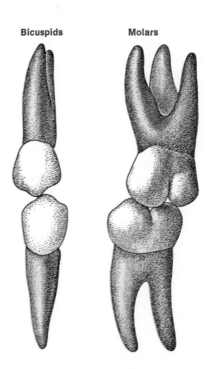

Bicuspids   Molars

Your Permanent Teeth

Here is a complete set of thirty-two permanent teeth. Which teeth do you have right now? Which ones have yet to grow in?

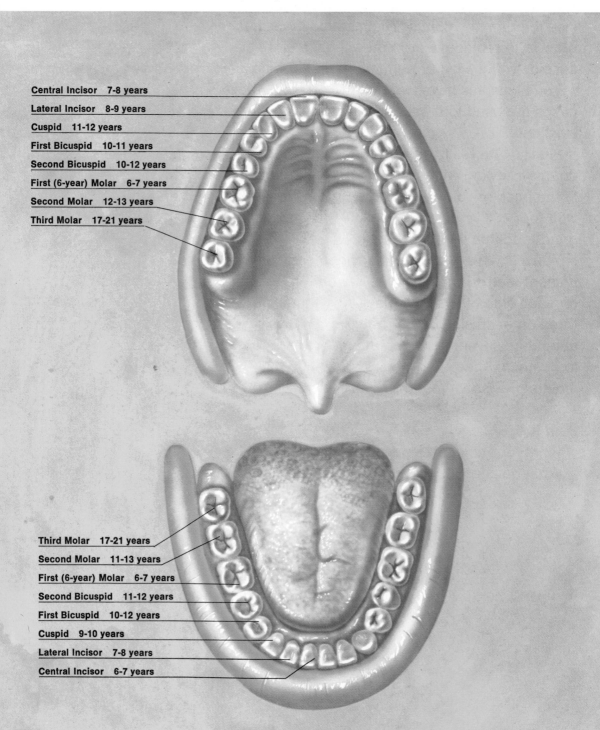

Central Incisor   7-8 years
Lateral Incisor   8-9 years
Cuspid   11-12 years
First Bicuspid   10-11 years
Second Bicuspid   10-12 years
First (6-year) Molar   6-7 years
Second Molar   12-13 years
Third Molar   17-21 years

Third Molar   17-21 years
Second Molar   11-13 years
First (6-year) Molar   6-7 years
Second Bicuspid   11-12 years
First Bicuspid   10-12 years
Cuspid   9-10 years
Lateral Incisor   7-8 years
Central Incisor   6-7 years

How Can You Take Good Care of Your Teeth?

Teacher's Notes
Students might use a hand mirror and the drawing on page 136 to find their six-year molars. They might also want to discover what other permanent teeth have come in.
Invite comments about pupils' own experiences with a dentist or a dental hygienist. What was done for their teeth? What tools were used? How do they feel about going to the dentist?
Glossary words: *calculus, cavity, dental hygienist, scaler, tartar*

Your permanent teeth have a general timetable for growing in. *(Now you know the answer to Riddle 2. Both your teeth and trains have time-tables!)* The first permanent teeth come in when you are about six years old. These teeth are called *six-year molars.* They do the heavy work of chewing while the primary teeth are being replaced.

Six-year molars also guide other permanent molars into proper place as they grow in. Why do you think these molars are often called "the most important teeth in the mouth"? Can you find the six-year molars on the opposite page?

No other teeth will grow in to take the place of your permanent teeth. So you should take good care of every one of them. When permanent teeth are lost, they can only be replaced by false teeth. False teeth are expensive. And usually they do not work as well as natural teeth.

Regular visits to the dentist help keep your teeth in good condition. The dentist checks your teeth for *cavities.* The dentist also checks for *tartar,* or *calculus.* Calculus is a hard, yellow sub-stance that forms on teeth. It can irritate the gums. Then the gums bleed.

The dentist removes calculus when he or she cleans the teeth. Sometimes a helper, or *dental hygienist,* does the cleaning. A dental tool called a *scaler* is used for cleaning. You can see this tool at the right. Has a dentist or a dental hygien-ist cleaned your teeth recently?

Dental mirror   **Scaler**

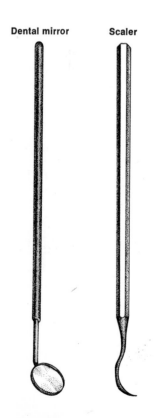

137

Flossing and Brushing the Teeth

Flossing and brushing your teeth helps remove *plaque* from them. Plaque is a sticky, colorless film of harmful *germs.* If plaque is not removed daily, it hardens and forms calculus.

Do you know what happens within minutes after you eat? Certain germs in plaque change foods, especially sweet foods, into *acids.* These acids begin cavities, or *tooth decay. (The word* decay *answers Riddle 3. Two letters that suggest a dental problem are DK!)* The acids dissolve tooth enamel and make holes in it. That is why you should floss and brush your teeth at least once a day.

Before brushing, you should use dental floss to remove plaque from between the teeth. Look at the pictures on the next page. How do you *floss* your teeth?

When brushing, use a toothbrush with a *flat* brushing surface and *soft* bristles. That kind of brush will reach all your teeth. And it will not injure your gums. Also tip the brush toward the gum line to remove plaque there.

Choose a toothpaste with an approved *fluoride* in it. Fluoride helps prevent cavities. Check the box to see that the toothpaste is accepted by the American Dental Association (ADA). At the left you see one way to brush the teeth. Can you show how to do it?

Now turn to pages 140–143 to find out more about tooth decay.

Sum It Up

Why is it important to take good care of your teeth?

How do you floss and brush the teeth?

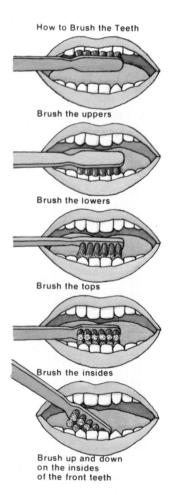

How to Brush the Teeth

Brush the uppers

Brush the lowers

Brush the tops

Brush the insides

Brush up and down on the insides of the front teeth

Flossing the Teeth

Wind about ½ meter of floss around each of your middle fingers.

Hold the floss between each thumb and forefinger. Allow about 3 centimeters of floss between them, to guide the floss.

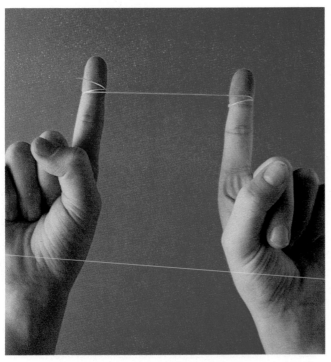

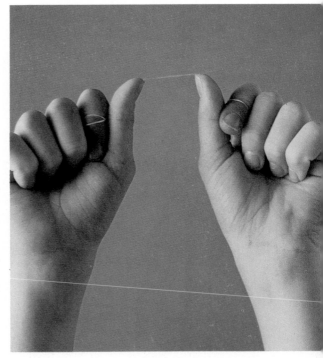

Hold the floss tightly. Move it back and forth to ease it between the gum and tooth.

Scrape the floss up and down against the side of each tooth. Use a clean part each time.

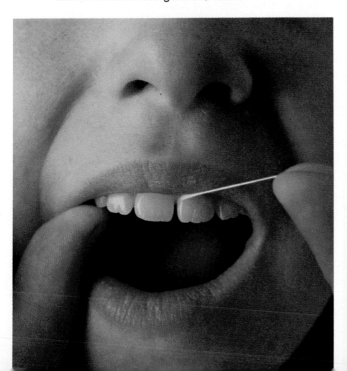

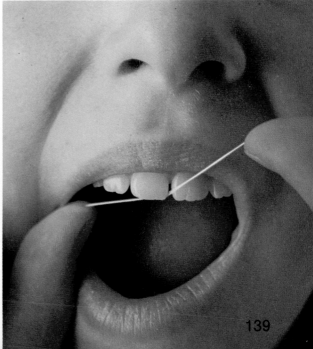

139

Tooth Decay
  Germs work on bits of food left on the teeth. Acids form that can dissolve tooth enamel.

After the enamel is dissolved, decay spreads into the dentin. This causes a hole, or cavity, in the tooth.

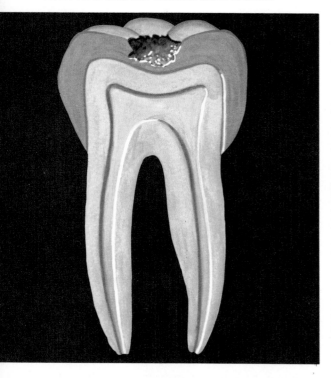

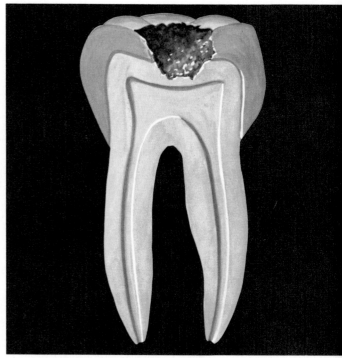

The cavity, if not repaired, spreads into the pulp. Pus, or an *abcess,* may form.

The dentist cleans out tooth decay. A filling of silver or other material is put in the tooth.

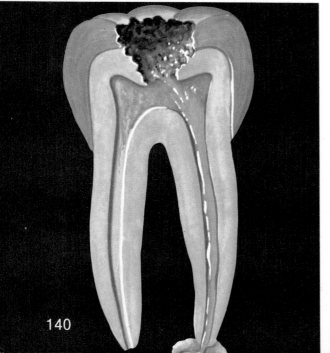

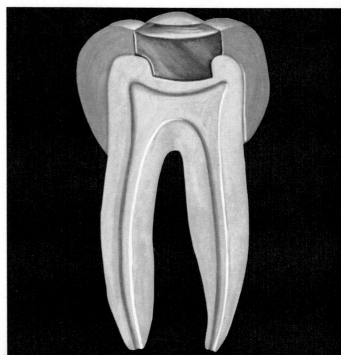

Here are some photographs of teeth with decay. You can see the start of decay in this bicuspid. Some enamel has been dissolved.

Now decay has spread into the dentin. You can see a small cavity here. A dentist can clean and fill this cavity.

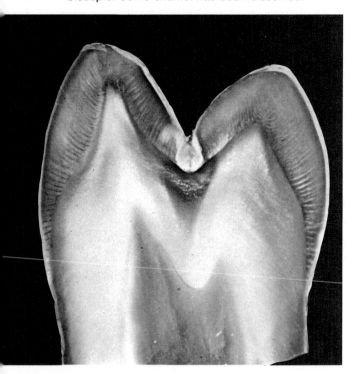

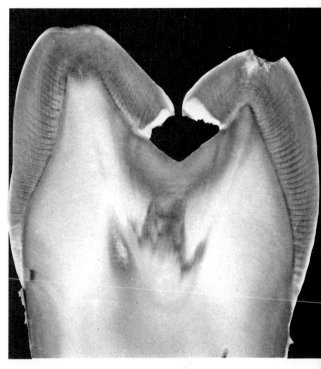

Decay has spread far into the dentin of this molar. Such decay may cause a toothache.

Decay has spread into the pulp of the incisor. This tooth may have to be pulled.

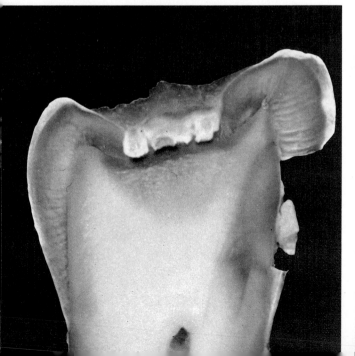

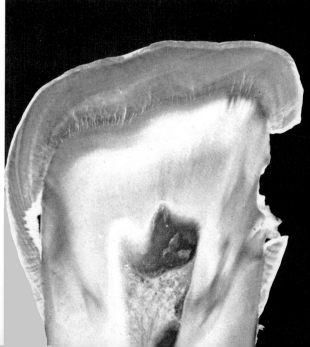

A Visit to the Dentist

1. Dentist's helper greets visitor.

2. Dentist fastens bib.

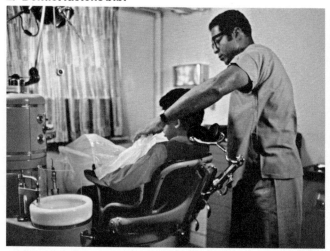

3. Dentist adjusts light.

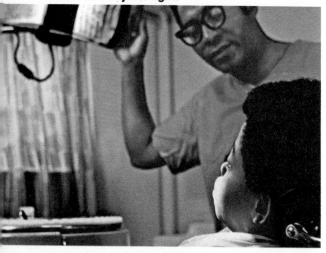

4. Dentist examines teeth.

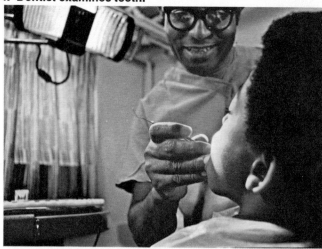

5. A cavity shows up in the mirror.

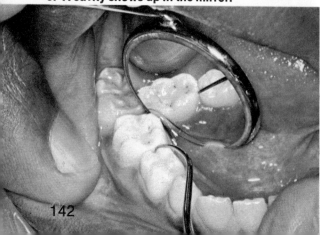

6. Dentist prepares cavity for filling.

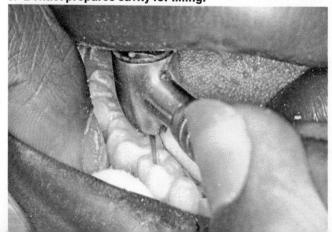

7. Mixed filling material is picked up.

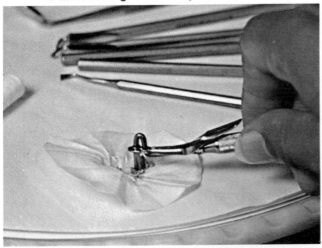

8. Filling is put in tooth.

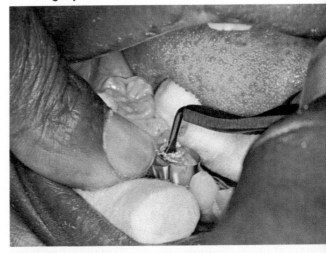

9. Excess filling material is scraped off.

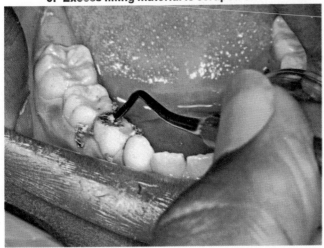

10. Bite is tested with new filling in place.

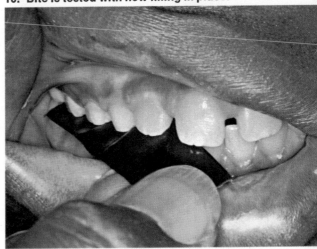

11. Filling material is given a final polishing.

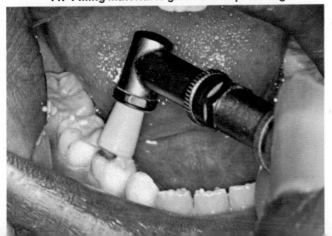

12. "Good bye. We'll see you soon."

143

ENJOY IT

Teacher's Notes

The painting here offers children a vivid opportunity to compare the equipment and methods of early dentists with those of today! See also page T34 for additional teaching suggestions.

Tooth Extraction, Theodore Rombouts, Museum of Fine Arts, Ghent.

Today, a dentist's office is a pleasant place. Teeth are cleaned there. And the dentist saves most teeth by repairing them.

But things were different long ago. Dentists pulled decayed teeth, instead of repairing them. And other people came to watch!

Here you can see a painting called *Tooth Extraction.* It was painted over three hundred years ago. What do you think about such old-time dentists?

HEALTH AROUND US

Teacher's Notes
"Health Around Us" is a recurring feature in this book and in this health series. At times, careers in the field of health will be highlighted. Here children learn about a dental specialist—the orthodontist.

See also page T34.

The young person you see here is under the care of an *orthodontist.* An orthodontist is a dentist who takes care of irregular or crowded teeth.

Sometimes primary teeth come out too soon. Teeth nearby may move over to fill part of the empty space. If that happens, the permanent teeth can grow into the wrong position.

The orthodontist knows how to help teeth grow into proper position. Metal bands, wire bars, rubber bands, and hooks may be used. These have to be tightened often. But slowly the out-of-place teeth are helped to grow into position. How long do you think it takes?

145

WRITE IT

There are lots of things you can write about teeth or the dentist. You might write about the painting on page 144. You might write about how you feel when you go to the dentist's. Or you might write some riddles about the teeth.

Here is what some boys and girls your age wrote. What will you write?

Teacher's Notes

Students should have a chance to express their feelings about visits to the dentist. Because of advances in modern dentistry, a good many youngsters have had no unpleasant experiences. They may, however, have had fear of what the dentist *might* do. Some students may want to write about things they *like* about dental visits. Be sure to give volunteers a chance to read aloud what they have written.

See also page T34 for additional teaching suggestions.

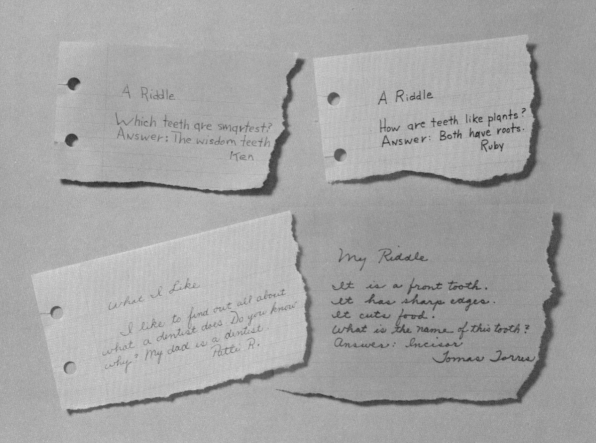

A Riddle

Which teeth are smartest?
Answer: The wisdom teeth
Ken

A Riddle

How are teeth like plants?
Answer: Both have roots.
Ruby

What I Like

I like to find out all about what a dentist does. Do you know why? My dad is a dentist.
Patti R.

My Riddle

It is a front tooth.
It has sharp edges.
It cuts food.
What is the name of this tooth?
Answer: Incisor
Tomas Torres

Things to Do

Teacher's Notes
Item 1: Answers to the puzzle are *cuspids, molars, bicuspids, incisors*
"Special Research" offers extra research or investigation activities for advanced or highly motivated students. See also page T34 for additional teaching suggestions.

1. Unscramble the letters below. Figure out the names of four shapes of teeth. Write the names. After each name, tell what that tooth does.

cusdips   cusdipsbi
larsmo   cisorsin

2. Make a poster that shows one good way to care for the teeth.

3. Be ready to tell the group about how a dentist or dental hygienist has helped you lately.

4. Bring some dental floss to school. Use it to demonstrate how to floss the teeth.

5. Work with others to make a play about a child's visit to the dentist.

6. See how many of these words you can spell. Look at each word. Then cover it and write it.

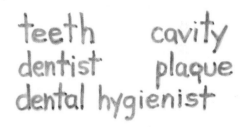

teeth   cavity
dentist   plaque
dental hygienist

Special Research

1. Find out about *disclosing tablets.* What are they? How do they help you know if you are brushing your teeth properly?

2. Make a report on the many kinds of work a dentist does. Here is a book that can help you:

Shay, Arthur. *What It's Like to Be a Dentist* (Reilly & Lee).

Can You Show What You Know?[1]

Teacher's Notes
Here behavioral objectives in the *cognitive* area are posed in childlike language directly to the children themselves. In turn, boys and girls give evidence by *observable behavior* of what they have learned.
Other hoped-for behavioral objectives lie chiefly in the less easily observed *affective* area—objectives that pertain to feelings, attitudes, and values.
Some of them are:
Practices what has been learned about care of the teeth.
Is aware of the effects of sweet foods on tooth decay.
Appreciates the many ways in which teeth help us.
Initiates independent research on teeth or the work of the dentist.
Develops some consciousness of the history of dentistry.

Page numbers show you where to look back in the chapter for information, if you need it.

1. List two reasons why you need your teeth. (131)
2. Name the four kinds of material that make up the teeth. (132)
3. Explain why the enamel of your teeth should be protected. (132)
4. Describe the four different kinds of teeth and what they do. (134–135)
5. Explain how you can help keep your teeth in good condition. (137)
6. Discuss *how* decay can be caused. (138)
7. Describe the kind of toothbrush that you should use. (138)
8. Demonstrate how to brush your teeth. (138)
9. Explain why teeth should be flossed. (138)
10. Tell *where* decay first starts in a tooth. (140)

[1] Behavioral objectives in the cognitive area are stated here directly to students themselves.

Review It

Page numbers show you where to look back in the chapter for information, if you need it.

1. Where are blood vessels and nerves found in a tooth? (132)

2. What is meant by the crown of a tooth? (132)

3. How many roots can a tooth have? (132)

4. What is plaque? (138)

5. How do sweet, sticky foods help start tooth decay? (138)

6. What is a good kind of toothpaste to use? (138)

7. What does the dentist do when he or she finds a cavity? (142–143)

8. How many incisors do you have in your mouth? (134)

Copy each numbered item from List A. After each item, write the letter and words from List B that best describe it. For example:

9. calculus   e. yellow substance that forms on teeth

List A

9. calculus
10. dental cavities
11. enamel
12. third molars
13. scaler

List B

a. white covering on tooth crown
b. tool for cleaning teeth
c. wisdom teeth
d. tooth decay
e. yellow substance that forms on teeth

Health Test for Chapter Five

Teacher's Notes
After students have taken the test and their papers have been scored, the test items can serve as guides for a summary discussion. Volunteers can read aloud their rewording of false statements.
(*Note:* "What Do You Think?" is a special feature that offers pupils a chance to evaluate some of their newly acquired knowledge.)

Copy each number on a piece of paper. After each number write the correct answer, *true* or *false*. Rewrite each false statement to make it true.

F 1. Enamel is very soft.

F 2. All teeth have two roots.

T 3. If tooth enamel is injured, no new enamel can ever be formed.

T 4. Tooth decay always begins on the outside of the tooth.

T 5. A dentist removes calculus with a tool called a scaler.

T 6. Incisors are in the front of the mouth.

T 7. The chewing surface of a bicuspid has two points.

T 8. Molars grind food into very, very tiny bits.

F 9. Dentin is found in the center of the tooth.

F 10. You will eventually have forty-two permanent teeth.

T 11. Six-year molars are some of your permanent teeth.

T 12. The dental hygienist is a worker who cleans teeth.

T 13. Cementum covers the root of a tooth.

T 14. Another name for calculus is tartar.

T 15. Flossing removes plaque from between the teeth.

T 16. There are blood vessels and nerves in the pulp of a tooth.

T 17. Use a toothbrush with soft bristles and a flat brushing surface.

T 18. Cut down on sweets if you want to help prevent tooth decay.

F 19. Calculus is good for the gums.

F 20. A person can remove calculus with a toothbrush.

Number of Answers	20
Number Right	_____
Score (Number Right × 5)	_____

What Do You Think?

In what ways do you think this chapter has helped you? Write your ideas on a piece of paper.

SCHOOL & HOME

Teacher's Notes
Special efforts are made in this book and in this health series to foster school-home communication.
It is hoped that some of the dental health information learned at school will be carried home by pupils. Full discussion of the ideas presented here will aid in motivating students to share their newly acquired dental-health knowledge with the family.

What are you going to do at home to help protect your teeth? What can you tell your family about ways to take care of the teeth?

You can also demonstrate the need for flossing the teeth. Here is a demonstration that shows how flossing removes plaque:

Cover one hand with a mixture of baking soda and water. Hold your fingers together.

Now use a toothbrush and water to remove the baking-soda mixture. Notice that the toothbrush will not remove material from between your fingers.

In the same way, a toothbrush cannot remove plaque from between the teeth. Only flossing removes plaque there.

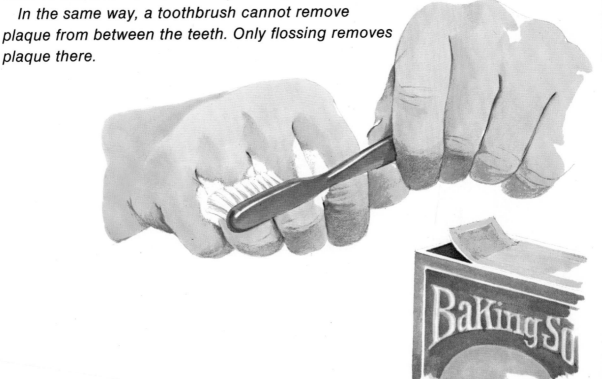

6 Finding Out About Diseases

What do you think is meant by "catching" a disease? What are some diseases that you can "catch"?

How do you think the body fights off diseases? What can *you* do to help?

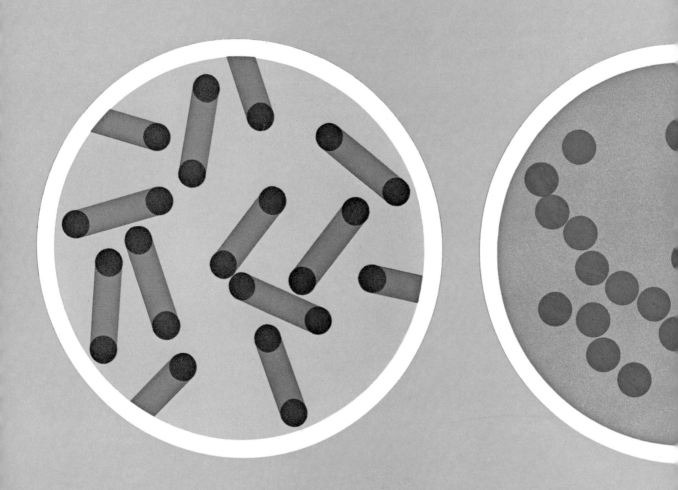

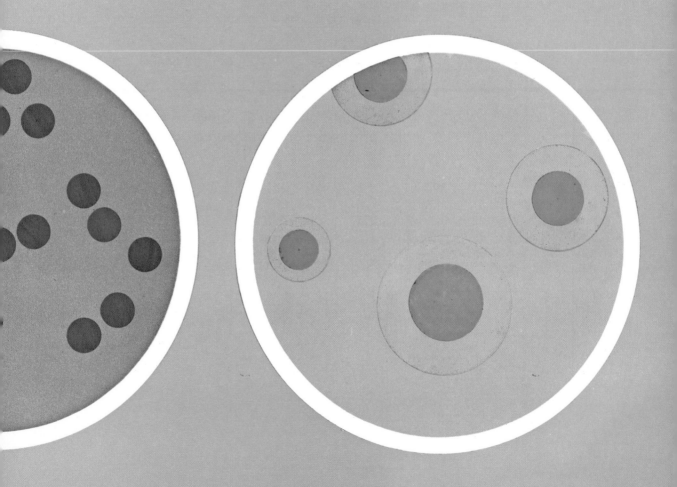

Teacher's Notes

See the Enrichment Suggestions for Chapter Six on page T35 of the Teacher's Supplement. See also the Reference Materials on page T43.

"Preview It" is a special feature that occurs at the beginning of each chapter in this book and in this health series. Here students do some *anticipating.* They skim over the main headings in the chapter. Most of these headings are, by design, study questions. Curiosities are aroused, and pupils are given a framework for the detailed information to follow.

Glossary word: *disease*

See also page T35 for additional teaching suggestions.

Preview It

Look quickly through this chapter. Try to find the four main questions that are asked. As you study the chapter, keep looking for answers. The answers will tell you something about diseases.

Here is a poem about one kind of disease that you sometimes "catch" from others. What do you think it is?

It doesn't breathe.
It doesn't smell.
It doesn't feel
So very well.

I am discouraged
With my nose;
The only thing it
Does is blows.

Now begin the chapter. Start by learning about colds and other *communicable diseases.*

What Is a Communicable Disease?

At times you may be ill with a cold. In a few days someone else in your family may get the cold too. The person may have "caught" the cold from you. How do you think this happens?

To find out, you need to know about *communicable diseases.* Such diseases are passed from one person to another. And they are caused by tiny *disease germs.*

Germs or *microbes* are everywhere. But they are so tiny that you need a microscope to see them. A microscope makes them look larger. Most of these microbes are harmless. But some cause diseases. These are disease germs.

If you have disease germs in your body, you can pass them to others. For example, suppose you have a cold. The cold germs may come out of your mouth or nose as you eat, talk, sneeze, or cough. Some cold germs may stay in the air. Others may settle on food or dishes.

Another person may breathe in the cold germs. Or the person may eat or drink from dishes with germs on them. Then that person may get your cold.

Teacher's Notes
Students can read to find out about communicable diseases and how they are "caught."
You might have students list all the things they learned on this page and the next about germs. You could also jot down their statements on the chalkboard.
(*Note:* Germs can also be spread by common use of such utensils as glasses and towels, by impure food or water, and by flies and other insects.)
Glossary words: *communicable disease, microbe*
See also page T35.

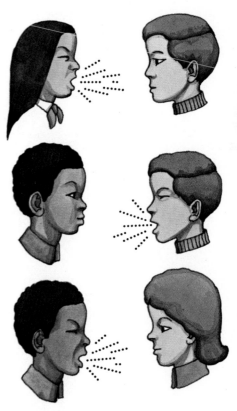

How are these boys and girls spreading disease germs? What might they do to help prevent the spread of such germs?

155

Germs can enter your body through the nose or mouth. Or they may enter through cuts in the skin. Once germs are in your body, they may multiply. They do this by dividing in half. Each half becomes a new germ.

Germs need a warm place to live and grow and multiply. They need a moist place. And they need food. The inside of your body gives them all of these things.

Suppose harmful germs of a certain kind get inside you and multiply. Then you may get sick. You get sick with the disease that kind of germ causes. Each communicable disease is caused by one kind of germ. For example, one kind of germ usually causes mumps. Another kind usually causes chicken pox.

Noncommunicable Diseases

Not all diseases are caused by germs. Some diseases cannot be passed from one person to another. Such diseases are *noncommunicable diseases.* They are caused by some difficulty within the body itself.

For example, *diabetes* is a noncommunicable disease. If a person has diabetes, the body cannot properly use the sugar in food. *High blood pressure* is another noncommunicable disease. With high blood pressure, the heart or blood vessels may not work as they should.

What other noncommunicable diseases do you know about?

Sum It Up

How can you "catch" a disease that is communicable?

How is a communicable disease different from a noncommunicable disease?

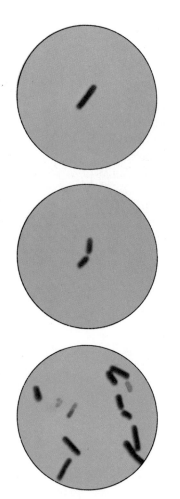

After a short time, what happened to the disease germ at the top?

156

What Are Some Main Groups of Disease Germs?

Bacteria are a group of germs that sometimes cause diseases. Bacteria are all around you. But only certain kinds are harmful. If the harmful kind get inside your body, they can cause diseases. For example, harmful bacteria can cause scarlet fever, "strep" sore throat, diphtheria, and whooping cough.

Look at the pictures below. These bacteria are greatly enlarged. What shapes do you see?

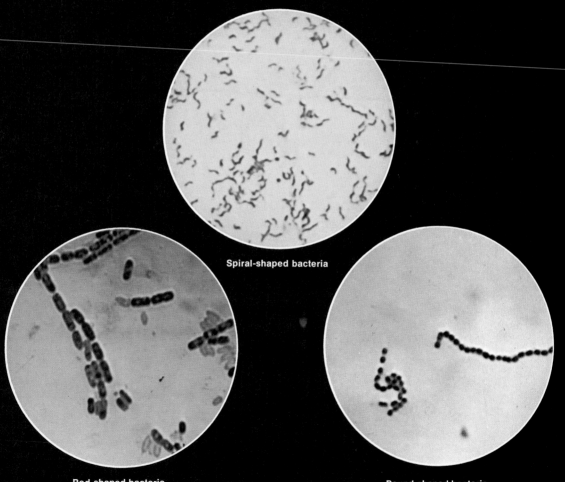

Spiral-shaped bacteria

Rod-shaped bacteria

Round-shaped bacteria

Viruses

Another group of disease germs are the *viruses.* They are very, very tiny. They are the tiniest germs of all. A special microscope must be used to see them. It is an *electron-microscope.*

Viruses can be found almost anywhere. Most of the viruses now known are harmful. They can cause diseases such as colds, flu, polio, mumps, and measles.

You can see some viruses below. Remember, they are enlarged thousands of times. How would you describe the ones you see here?

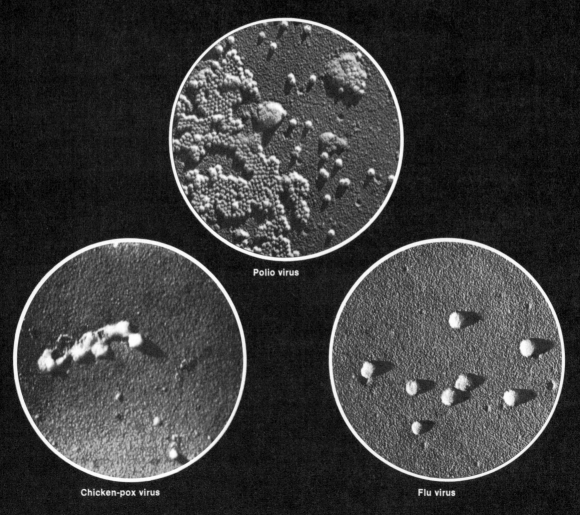

Polio virus

Chicken-pox virus

Flu virus

_____

Name

I   see

The

Name

I see

The

Protozoans

Other germs that can make you ill are the *protozoans.* Most of these germs live in water. And most are harmless. But some can cause an infection in the intestines. Some can cause *malaria.* And some can cause *sleeping sickness.*

Protozoans are larger than other germs. Some harmful ones are shown below. They are greatly enlarged. What differences do you see in these protozoans?

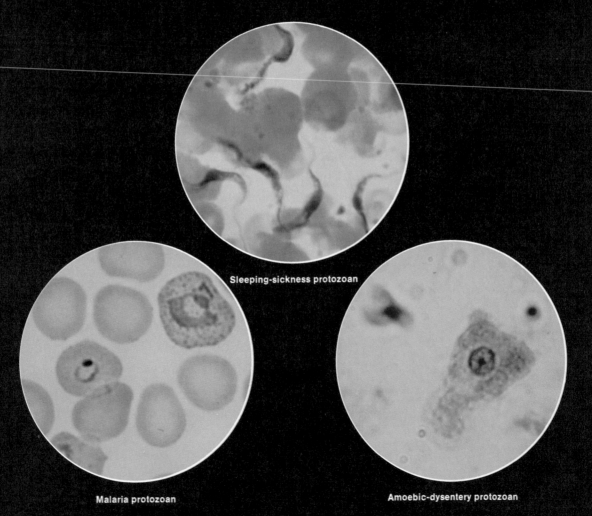

Sleeping-sickness protozoan

Malaria protozoan

Amoebic-dysentery protozoan

How Does the Body Fight Off Disease Germs?

Many disease germs never get into the body. Your skin keeps them out. Germs can enter through a cut, though. So always wash a cut with soap and water. Then cover the cut with a clean bandage. How do you think this can help?

Some germs do get into the body with the air you breathe. But tiny hairs in your nose catch many of them. Or the germs may be trapped by *mucus.* Mucus is a sticky fluid that keeps the lining of your nose and throat moist. Mucus also has a germ-killing substance in it. If germs do enter the lungs, they are likely to be coughed up.

Some disease germs get into the body with food you eat. But most are killed by *saliva* or by stomach juices.

At times, disease germs do get past your nose and throat. Or they are not killed by saliva and stomach juices. Then certain cells in your blood fight off the germs. These are the *white blood cells.* They form a wall around the germs. The wall keeps the germs from spreading. Then the white blood cells kill the germs by "eating" them.

Sometimes disease germs are *not* blocked off. They are *not* killed by white blood cells. Then the germs start to divide and grow. Soon there are more germs. Some of the germs produce substances that injure body cells. These substances may also keep the cells from working properly. When that happens, you feel sick.

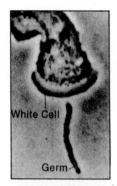

White Cell

Germ

What is happening to the germ?

160

Antibodies

Your body has other ways to fight off disease germs. It forms *antibodies.* Antibodies are substances that circulate in the blood. They help white blood cells destroy disease germs.

The body makes a special kind of antibody to fight each kind of disease germ. After you get over a disease, some antibodies stay in your blood. Some stay a short time. Some stay for many years. Some stay a lifetime.

If germs of the same disease enter your body again, the antibodies are there to fight off the germs. For example, if you have had chicken pox, you are not likely to get it again. You probably have developed lifetime *immunity* to that disease. But for colds and flu, there is little or no immunity period.

Helpful Drugs

Sometimes your body needs help fighting disease germs. Some of the germs that get into your body can be killed or greatly weakened by *medicines.* Most of these medicines are the *antibiotic drugs.*

Antibiotic drugs are useful. But they are powerful. They should only be prescribed for serious kinds of diseases. Often it is better to let your body fight off colds or flu than to depend on drugs.

Only a doctor can write a prescription for an antibiotic drug. The drug is prescribed just for the sick person. And it should not be given to anyone else. You must also take the drug exactly according to directions. Why is this important?

Teacher's Notes

After preliminary discussion, you might ask:

"What are antibodies and what do they do?" (See Glossary.)

"For what diseases have you developed immunity by having them?"

"What is meant by immunity?" (See Glossary.)

"What are some diseases for which the period of immunity is quite short?"

Also discuss the uses of antibiotics. Emphasize the care that must be taken with them. See if pupils can name some of the common antibiotics (penicillin, streptomycin, tetracycline).

(*Note:* Special features in the margin, such as "Something to Think About," are designed to keep children active, interested, and alert throughout each chapter.)

Glossary words: *antibody, antibiotic, immunity, medicine*

Something to Think About

Sometimes it is said that the body has "soldiers" to help protect it. What are these "soldiers"?

The word *antibiotic* means "against living things." What living things do antibiotic drugs fight against?

Teacher's Notes

In a preliminary discussion see what ideas students have about "shots." Later, talk over how vaccines work to give people immunity against certain communicable diseases. Use the diagram in the margin to help you. You might also ask:

"How is polio vaccine usually given today?" (By mouth—in a syrup or on a sugar cube.)

"What is meant by boosters?" (See Glossary.)

Glossary words: *booster, vaccine, whooping cough*

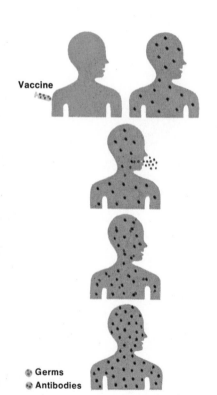

Vaccine

🦠 **Germs**
🦠 **Antibodies**

Vaccines cause your body to make antibodies. The antibodies fight off germs of a communicable disease.

Vaccines

Having a disease or taking drugs can be a dangerous way to fight off some disease germs. Fortunately, there is something else that can be done. Your body can be made to produce its own protection against different disease germs. *Vaccines* can be injected into the body. Or they can be given by mouth. Vaccines cause your body to make protective antibodies.

Vaccines differ from one another. Some vaccines have disease germs in them that have been killed. The vaccine against *whooping cough* is an example. You are not harmed when these killed germs are injected into your body. But your body reacts by producing antibodies to fight off whooping cough.

Some vaccines contain disease germs that are alive, but greatly weakened. Polio vaccine is an example. When the weakened germs enter your body, they usually do not make you sick at all. But the germs cause your body to make antibodies to fight polio.

The protection given by some vaccines may not last too long. It may not last as long as if you had had the disease. So it may be necessary to have *booster* doses or shots later. You need boosters so that your body will always have the antibodies to fight off certain germs. What boosters have you had recently?

Sum It Up

What have you found out about bacteria, viruses, and protozoans?

What are three or four ways your body fights off diseases?

How can vaccines help fight certain diseases?

162

HEALTH AROUND US

Teacher's Notes
"Health Around Us" is a recurring feature in this book and in this health series. On this page students learn some of the methods used to vaccinate against serious diseases. See also page T36.

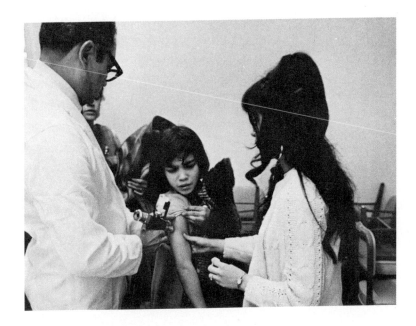

People are given vaccines to *immunize* or to protect them against certain diseases.

There are different ways to give vaccines. They can be *injected.* Or many can be given by *mouth.* Sometimes a *vaccinating gun* is used to inject a vaccine.

The vaccinating gun works very fast. It can vaccinate fifty children without a refill. Here you can see a doctor using a vaccinating gun.

Why might a doctor want to give a vaccine in this way?

Additional pages have been devoted to immunization because declining levels of immunity are one of this country's serious disease prevention problems. Recent outbreaks of diphtheria, for example, have been attributed to declining immunity in the population. Routine immunization could prevent such occurrences.

Glossary word: *diphtheria*
See also page T36 for additional teaching suggestions.

Why Do People Still "Catch" Dangerous Diseases?

There are vaccines for many serious diseases. There are vaccines for polio, mumps, measles, diphtheria, tetanus, rubella, and whooping cough. Yet both children and grown-ups still get some of these diseases.

Many people haven't been immunized against the serious diseases. The vaccines are there. But people have not been vaccinated. Or people may not have had boosters as needed.

Children should be immunized against all the diseases named above in the preschool years. But the Public Health Service tells us that one out of every three preschool children is not properly immunized against serious diseases.

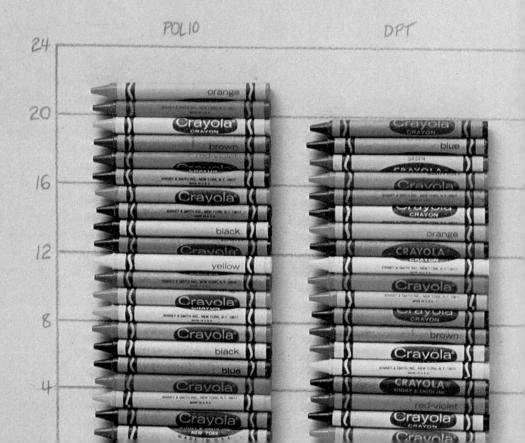

Maybe you wonder if *you* are protected against these diseases. How can you find out? Remember that you can be immunized now if you weren't properly immunized earlier.

Your group might want to do what another group did. This group of twenty-four schoolchildren made a graph. The graph shows how well they are immunized. You can see the graph below.

What information does the graph give you? What conclusions can you draw from it?

How might your group go about making such a graph?

Sum It Up

Why is it important to be immunized against certain diseases?

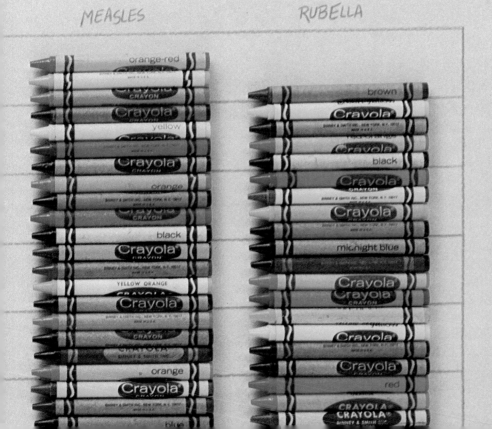

MEASLES   RUBELLA

Good Health Practices
The poster below suggests one thing you can do to protect *yourself* against disease germs.
What message would you put on this poster?

Here is a poster that suggests something you
can do to help protect *others* from disease germs.
What message would you put on this poster?

WRITE IT

Think of a time when you were ill. How did you feel? What problems did the illness cause for you? What problems did it cause for others? Here is what some children wrote.
What will you write?

Teacher's Notes
If students have trouble writing their ideas about illness, various "starters" might be suggested. For example:
I don't like to be sick because. . . .
When I am sick, I like. . . .
When someone is sick at our house, we always. . . .
See also page T36 for additional teaching suggestions.

Happiness

Happiness is
NOT
GETTING
SICK!
by
George Sifco

MEASLES

I hate measles.

They are little red dots

That get on your face.

You cannot get them off with an eraser.

You have to wait and wait and wait.

You can't go to school

You have to sit in bed

And read the newspaper or something.

Maria

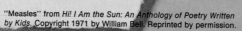

"Measles" from *Hi! I Am the Sun: An Anthology of Poetry Written by Kids.* Copyright 1971 by William Bell. Reprinted by permission.

Things to Do

Teacher's Notes
Item 1: The plastic bags that contain the potato slices should be incinerated. It is possible that some very harmful bacteria may have been cultured. Caution should be used.
"Special Research" activities are for advanced or highly motivated students. See also page T36 for additional teaching suggestions.

1. To find out if there are germs on your fingers and in your coughs or sneezes, here is something to try.

Put three slices of cooked potato on three small, clean saucers.

Have someone rub a finger over the potato on the first saucer. Label it.

Have someone cough on the potato on the second saucer. Label it.

Have someone sneeze on the potato on the third saucer. Label it.

Put each saucer in a clear plastic bag and seal it with tape.

Look at the potato slices each day.

If any germs appear on the potato slices, you will see large clumps. Each of these clumps will contain millions of germs.

Do not uncover the dishes at any time. Why?

2. Try to explain this slogan: *Cover the sneeze, prevent disease.*

3. Find out what the *pus* is that you may see around a cut or sore.

4. If you want to learn more about bacteria, look for books in the school or public library. Here is an easy book you might like:

Frahm, Anne. *The True Book of Bacteria* (Childrens Press).

5. See what you can find out about the *molds* you see on stale bread or fruits that are spoiling.

Special Research

1. Use an encyclopedia to find out about the World Health Organization (WHO). How does this organization help fight diseases?

2. Prepare a report about a non-communicable disease such as *lung cancer* or *chronic bronchitis* or *emphysema.* Be sure to tell what cigarette smoking may have to do with these diseases. Here is a book that may help:

Madison, Arnold. *Smoking and You* (Messner).

Can You Show What You Know?[1]

Teacher's Notes

Here behavioral objectives in the *cognitive* area are posed in childlike language directly to the children themselves. In turn, boys and girls give evidence by *observable behavior* of what they have learned.

Other hoped-for behavioral objectives lie chiefly in the less easily observed *affective* area—objectives that pertain to feelings, attitudes, and values. Some of them are:

Develops some awareness of how communicable diseases can be spread.

Realizes the need to try and protect others from catching a communicable disease he or she may have.

Is alert to ways to protect oneself from communicable diseases.

Develops some awareness of declining levels of immunity among children in this country.

Page numbers show you where to look back in the chapter for information, if you need it.

1. Explain what a communicable disease is. (155)

2. Tell how a person may "catch" a communicable disease. (155)

3. List three things germs need to live and grow and multiply. (156)

4. Explain the difference between a communicable and a noncommunicable disease. (156)

5. Name three main groups of disease germs. (157–159)

6. Tell about four or five of the body's defenses against diseases. (160–161)

7. Explain how vaccines can help protect you from certain diseases. (162)

8. Tell why children still get dangerous diseases such as polio and measles. (164)

[1] Behavioral objectives in the cognitive area are stated here directly to students themselves.

Review It

Teacher's Notes

"Review It" is a feature that occurs at the end of each chapter in this book and in this health series. It gives children a chance to think over what they have learned, to summarize, and to store away important ideas. Page references after each item make this review page a self-help one. However, group discussion can be a valuable adjunct.

Page numbers show you where to look back in the chapter for information, if you need it.

1. How do germs multiply inside your body? (156)

2. What are some ways you can "catch" a cold or some other communicable disease? (155)

3. Suppose someone in your family has high blood pressure. Can you "catch" this disease? Why or why not? (156)

4. What happens in your body after the vaccine against whooping cough is injected? (162)

5. For what purpose are antibiotic drugs given? What care must be taken with such drugs? (161)

6. What should you do about a small cut on the skin? (160)

7. What does being immunized against a disease mean? (163)

Copy each numbered item from List A. After each item, write the letter and words from List B that best describe it. For example:

8. antibodies   f. substances in blood that kill or weaken disease germs

List A

8. antibodies
9. diabetes
10. measles
11. protozoans
12. vaccines
13. viruses

List B

a. large germs that live mostly in water
b. communicable disease
c. tiniest germs of all
d. substance containing killed or weakened germs
e. noncommunicable disease
f. substances in blood that kill or weaken disease germs

Health Test for Chapter Six

Teacher's Notes
After students have taken the test and their papers have been scored, the test items can serve as guides for a summary discussion. Volunteers can read aloud their wording of the multiple-choice statements.
(*Note:* "What Do You Think?" is a special feature that offers pupils a chance to evaluate some of their newly acquired knowledge.)

Copy each number on a piece of paper. After the number write the letter that goes with the *best* answer choice.

1. The kind of germ that causes whooping cough (a) causes other diseases too, (b) causes only whooping cough, (c) causes polio as well.

2. A communicable disease is always caused by (a) mucus, (b) vaccines, (c) disease germs.

3. Some common germs are (a) bacteria, (b) antibiotics, (c) antibodies.

4. A noncommunicable disease is caused by (a) disease germs, (b) a difficulty within the body, (c) a vaccine.

5. The cells in the blood that help fight off disease germs are the (a) red blood cells, (b) white blood cells, (c) antibiotics.

6. Protozoans are found (a) in everyone's saliva, (b) mostly in water, (c) only in the air.

7. Substances that are produced by the body and that help white cells kill disease germs are (a) antibodies, (b) antibiotics, (c) immunities.

8. Three main groups of germs that cause diseases are (a) high blood pressure, diabetes, and flu (b) bacteria, protozoans, and viruses; (c) measles, mumps, and polio.

9. Vaccines are useful because they cause your body to make protective (a) mucus, (b) viruses, (c) antibodies.

10. Some disease germs are kept out of the body by (a) cuts in the skin, (b) the skin, (c) red blood cells.

Number of Answers	10
Number Right	____
Score (Number Right × 10)	____

What Do You Think?

What did you learn in this chapter that you think is important? Write your answer on a piece of paper.

SCHOOL & HOME

Teacher's Notes

Special efforts are made in this book and in this health series to foster school-home communication. Here students have an opportunity to decode and share a health message about disease with their families. Answer to health message: *Wash a small cut with soap and water at once.*

Suppose you get a communicable disease, such as a cold or the flu. What things can you do at home to keep from spreading the disease? You may want to talk over your ideas with members of your family.

If you haven't done so already, you may want to check at home about diseases you are immunized against. Check about boosters too.

Did you know that you are not so likely to get a communicable disease if you are healthy? Your body fights off diseases better when you are in good health. What are some things that can help keep you healthy? What are you doing at home to stay healthy?

Here is something else you can do. Decode the health message below.

Write the message on a piece of paper and take it home. Read the message to the family. What does it say? Why do you think the message is important?

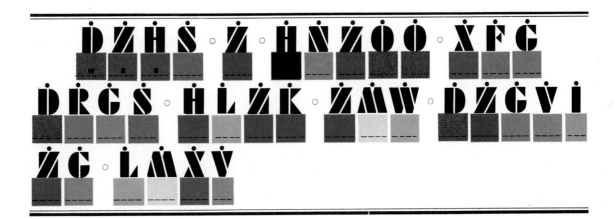

Key to Code

A B C D E F G H I J K L M N O P Q R S T U V W X Y Z
z y x w v u t s r q p o n m l k j i h g f e d c b a

173

7 Thinking About Community Health

How would you describe a person who is healthy?

Now suppose you were asked to describe a *community* that is healthy. What would you say? What do you think people can do to keep a community healthy?

175

Preview It

You need certain things to stay alive and healthy. You need air to breathe, water to drink, food to eat, and housing to shelter you.

But if you are to be as healthy as possible, you need more. You need *clean* air to breathe. You need *pure* water to drink. You need food that is *safe* to eat. And you need housing that *meets your family's needs*. You and your family can't get all these things by yourselves. You need the help of other people in your community.

To protect your health, your community has many problems to solve. Look quickly through this chapter. Find the main questions that are asked. What are some community health problems that the questions suggest? As you read the chapter, try to learn more about these problems.

Now begin the chapter. Find out who is in charge of looking after the health of a community.

What Does a Health Department Do?

The main job of the health department is to improve public health conditions. A health department may be large or small. It may be a city or county department. In any case, the main services are the same.

Perhaps you know about some things the health department does. Here are some things boys and girls your age have said.

"Sometimes a nurse from the health department comes to help a family when someone is sick."

"In our community there is a well-baby clinic. Mothers can take their babies to the clinic for health checkups."

"The health department has pamphlets about health for people to read."

"The health department sometimes has special immunization programs. The immunizations keep us from getting measles and other diseases."

"The health department has sanitarians. *These people inspect grocery stores and restaurants to see that food is clean and safe for us to eat."*

What other things do *you* know about the health department?

You can learn more by looking at the pictures on pages 178 and 179. What information do these pictures give?

Teacher's Notes

Use the title to start off preliminary conversation. Pupils can then study this page and the pictures on pages 178–179 for information. In the follow-up discussion other functions of a community health department might be mentioned. (For example, health departments help carry out rat-control programs and post signs, such as No Dogs Allowed.)

(*Note:* Special features in the margin, such as "Do You Know?" are designed to keep children active and alert.)

Glossary word: *sanitarian*

See also page T37 for additional teaching suggestions.

Do You Know?

Does your health department, or some other community group, do anything to help young people who have been unwisely experimenting with drugs? How can you find out?

The Health Department at Work

Public health nurses show families how to care for the sick or for a new baby.

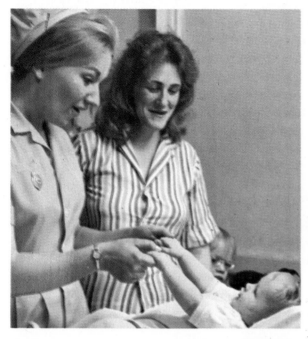

People in health-department laboratories test samples of public water supplies to be sure the water is safe to drink.

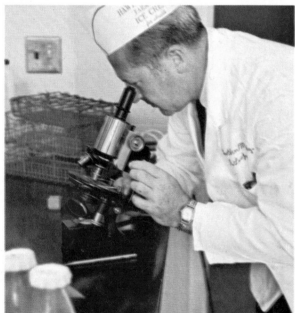

Health department workers test food in grocery stores and restaurants to make sure that it is safe to eat.

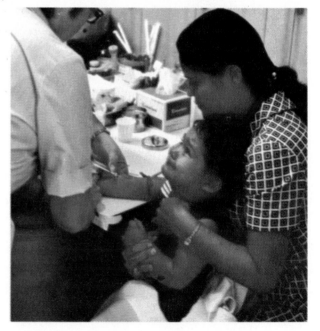

Public health workers immunize people to prevent diseases like diphtheria, whooping cough, polio, and measles.

Sanitarians inspect food. They check to see that it is prepared and sold in ways that are safe and sanitary.

Sanitarians also check to see that places like beaches, pools, alleys, and public washrooms are clean.

Health department workers check for air pollution. Dirt in the jar tells workers how much has fallen out of the air.

The health department keeps records of births, deaths, marriages, and cases of communicable diseases. How might such information help?

179

What Can Be Done About Air Pollution?

Dirty, or *polluted* air is a community health problem. Air pollution is especially bothersome in cities. But it is becoming a problem everywhere.

Air becomes polluted in many ways. You may already know that cars pollute the air. In fact, cars, trucks, buses, and airplanes are among the worst polluters. They cause pollution by sending partly burned gases into the air. The gases come out of exhaust pipes.

Air can also be polluted by smoke from the burning of trash and leaves. Air is polluted by smoke from factories. And it is polluted by gases from factories.

Air can be polluted even though you cannot see the pollution. Some of the harmful gases that pour into the air are invisible. You may not smell the gases either. But there are special instruments that can detect these gases.

Damage Caused by Air Pollution

Dirt, smoke, and gases in the air may be carried away by wind and by air currents. But sometimes the air is quite still. Then smoke and gases are trapped near the earth. And a blanket of *smog* may settle over us.

Smog can irritate the eyes, nose, throat, and lungs. Smog can also make it difficult for some people to breathe.

If you breathe polluted air year after year, it can cause changes in the lungs. These changes keep the lungs from working properly. Air pollution can cause, or make worse, diseases like *emphysema* and *bronchitis.* Such diseases usually affect older people. But everyone may feel uncomfortable and lack energy when air is polluted.

Air pollution can also rot and soil clothes. It can rust metals and discolor paint. And it can damage plant life. It costs billions of dollars each year to repair air-pollution damage.

What sources of air pollution are shown in this picture?

Finding Ways to Fight Air Pollution

How can people in a community work to cut down on air pollution? One way is to stop the burning of trash. Many communities forbid the burning of trash or leaves by families.

Some communities burn garbage in special furnaces, or *incinerators,* that do not pollute the air. Other communities bury garbage. Still other communities burn garbage, along with fuels like coal, to generate electricity. The electricity is used for heat and light in a community. And someday machines may be used to change garbage into building materials.

Today, many factories use devices to reduce the smoke, dust, or harmful gases coming from their smokestacks.

Harmful gases from exhausts of cars are being reduced by special anti-pollution devices. Special kinds of gasoline can also help reduce air pollution. More efficient engines can help too.

Some families are helping by using cars less and walking more. How does *your* family help in reducing air pollution?

How clean is the air in your community? How might you find out?

Sum It Up

What pollutes the air we breathe?

How can air pollution affect our health?

What damage can air pollution do?

What can be done to help cut down on air pollution?

Teacher's Notes

After pupils have studied the page, discuss ways of reducing air pollution. You might ask:

"What can car manufacturers do to help eliminate air pollution?" (Build ever better devices to reduce air pollution.)

"What can families who own cars do?" (Use cars as little as possible, join car pools, use public transportation when possible.)

(*Note:* "Sum It Up" is a feature that occurs at intervals throughout each chapter of this book and of others in the health series. Pupils can use this study aid to review important ideas learned in the preceding pages.)

Glossary word: *incinerator*

See also page T37 for additional teaching suggestions.

Books to Read

Look in your school or public library for books about air pollution. Here are some good ones:

Bloome, Enid P. *The Air We Breathe* (Doubleday).

Elliott, Sarah M. *Our Dirty Air* (Messner).

Tannenbaum, Beulah, and Stillman, Myra. *Clean Air* (McGraw-Hill).

What Can Be Done About Water Pollution?

Water pollution is caused by dumping wastes into lakes, rivers, and other bodies of water.

Every time you open the drain in your sink, washbowl, or bathtub, you send water down a drainpipe. The drainpipe leads into sewer pipes. Wastes from garbage disposals and toilets are sent down drainpipes into sewer pipes too. All these wastes are called *sewage.*

In some communities household wastes are carried through sewer pipes to nearby waterways. The wastes are dumped *untreated* into nearby lakes, rivers, or streams.

Industries, too, may pollute water by pouring wastes into it.

Harmful wastes may also get into the soil or drain off fields that have been sprayed with *pesticides.* Pesticides are often used to kill insects and weeds in cities or on farms.

Teacher's Notes

Discuss some of the sources of water pollution explained on page 185. Then ask:

"How else can a body of water be polluted?" (People might dump such things as old tires, cans, bottles, boots, and papers into the water.)

"What is the chief purpose of a sewage-treatment plant?" (Point out that some communities have plants that are outdated and give sewage only a one-stage treatment; other communities give sewage a two-stage treatment; the most modern and effective plants give sewage a three-step treatment. See if pupils can learn more about the sewage-treatment plant in their community.)

Glossary words: *pesticide, sewage*

Making Water Safe to Use

Polluted lakes and other waterways are often a community's source for drinking water. Polluted water can spread many diseases. So people in communities must do something to make the water safe to use.

Many communities have *waste-treatment plants.* Sewage is piped to the waste-treatment plants *before* it is dumped into nearby waters. At a waste-treatment plant, solid materials are removed from sewage. Chemicals are used to kill most disease-causing bacteria. Then the water is returned to lakes and rivers or stored.

Some waste-treatment plants do a better job than others. And not all communities yet have these plants.

Industries can help reduce water pollution too. Many of them now treat their wastes before dumping them into waterways.

How does sewage get to the sewage-treatment plant from its source?

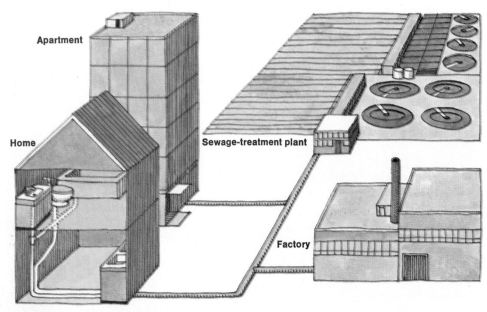

Apartment

Home

Sewage-treatment plant

Factory

186

Most communities also have *water-treatment plants.* Water is piped to the plants from nearby waterways or wells. Water may even be piped in from storage places, or *reservoirs,* a hundred miles or more away.

At the water-treatment plant, water is treated in various ways to kill harmful germs. The water is filtered through sand and gravel to remove dirt. Then the water is sprayed into the air to purify it further. Now the water is safe enough for the community to use.

Sum It Up

How does water get polluted?

How can polluted water affect the health of the community?

What can communities do to cut down on water pollution?

Teacher's Notes

After study of this page, guide a summary discussion with questions such as these:

"Why do people in a community care if their water sources are polluted?"

"What, besides danger to people's health, are some drawbacks of having a polluted body of water near a community?" (It looks and smells bad; it may no longer be used for swimming or fishing.)

"What is the chief purpose of a water-treatment plant? How is it different from a sewage-treatment plant?"

"How can water pollution be reduced?"

You might also see if anyone knows the source of the community water supply and the location of the sewage- and water-treatment plants.

Glossary word: *reservoir*

See also page T38 for additional teaching suggestions.

How does water get from a water-treatment plant to buildings in the community?

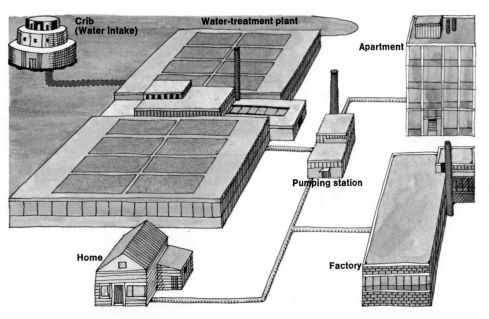

Crib (Water intake)

Water-treatment plant

Apartment

Pumping station

Home

Factory

What Can Be Done to Prevent Food Pollution?

Germs of many common diseases are spread by impure food and drink. Some examples of these diseases are tuberculosis, "septic" sore throat, and one kind of food poisoning.

Food can easily be polluted. Sometimes people handle food with unclean hands. Or they may cough or sneeze into foods. Then disease-causing germs are passed along to people who eat the foods. People who are sick should never work where food is being prepared or served.

Rats, mice, flies, and cockroaches spread diseases too. They get onto foods and spread dirt and germs.

Sanitarians check to see if sanitary methods of food-handling and food storage are used. They also teach workers sanitary guides for handling food.

You can see some of these guides on page 190. Which guides should you also use at home?

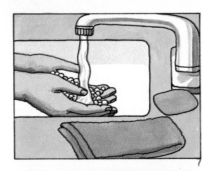

Wash hands with soap and hot water *before* handling food. Wash hands after you use a handkerchief and after you use the toilet.

Wash dishes, silverware, glasses, and cooking utensils in very hot, soapy water. Change the dishwater often. Rinse items with boiling water.

Touch only the *outside* of clean cups and glasses. Pick up clean spoons, forks, and knives by using the *handles.*

Keep all foods that spoil easily in a refrigerator of some kind.

Use cups and plates that are free of cracks or chipped places. Germs can grow there.

HEALTH AROUND US

Teacher's Notes
"Health Around Us" is a recurring feature in this book and in this health series. Here students have a chance to see and think about the effects of water pollution on a community. See also page T38.

A community health department has been at work here. How can you tell?

Polluted water can be unpleasant as well as unsafe for a community. Such water often looks bad, smells bad, and is full of harmful germs. And people may not be able to use the water for such things as swimming and fishing.

What can people in a community do to work for clean water?

What Are Some Housing Problems?

In some communities there is not enough proper housing for people. Some people may have to live in crowded, unsafe houses or apartments.

Some buildings are not safe from fires. Others have mice, fleas, cockroaches, and rats in them. Such pests pollute foods, spread disease germs, and may bite children.

Public health departments help control rats by using poisons and rat traps. But people must help, too, by keeping garbage in covered cans.

Often buildings are too close together. There are not enough yards and play areas for children. And there are no restful places with trees and grass for everyone's enjoyment.

People in communities can try to improve unhealthy, unsafe buildings and neighborhoods.

What has been done here to make this a more pleasant place to live?

What Can Be Done About Litter?

Litter is a kind of pollution too. Litter on the streets, in parks, and in other public places is unsanitary. Such litter can also affect the way people feel. How does it make *you* feel?

In many communities it is against the law to drop old papers and other trash on public property.

Look at the picture here. What has caused all this litter? How could it have been prevented?

What does your community do to make it easier for people to prevent litter?

What does your school do?

What can your group at school do about litter on the playground?

How would you describe a "litterbug"?

195

Where Will All the Trash and Garbage Go?

Every day in this country people throw away amazing amounts of garbage and trash. Make it a point this week to observe how much garbage and trash your family throws away.

There are many kinds of trash and garbage. For example, there are food wastes. These include fruit and vegetable peelings, chicken and meat bones, coffee grounds, and uneaten foods of various kinds.

There is also the packaging that foods come in. This includes cans, boxes, jars, bags, bottles, and wrappings. And there are old newspapers, magazines, cardboard boxes, paper towels and tissues, and gift wrappings.

Many other worn-out things are thrown away too. They may include old clothes, old radios, old car tires, and broken toys.

What else can you think of? How might some of these things be reused or *recycled*?

Some Ways a Community Can Dispose of Solid Wastes

Trash and garbage are often called *solid wastes.* What happens to these wastes after they are picked up by community garbage trucks?

Some communities take the solid wastes to *open dumps.* The dumps are usually in out-of-the-way places. Open dumps look ugly and smell bad. Flies, mice, and rats breed there. And if trash is burned in open dumps, it causes air pollution.

Other communities use the *sanitary landfill.* Trucks take the garbage to low, outlying areas. Machines spread the wastes over the land and pack them down. Chemicals are added to keep rats, mice, and flies from breeding. Then a layer of earth is spread over the garbage.

When the landfill is full, a thick layer of earth is put down. Trees and grass are planted. Parks, playgrounds, or golf courses may be built on the landfill. But many communities are running out of land to use.

What happens to garbage once it gets to a sanitary landfill?

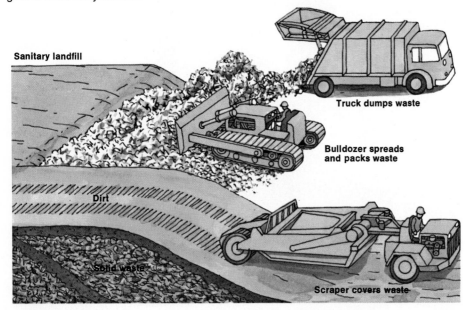

Sanitary landfill

Truck dumps waste

Bulldozer spreads and packs waste

Dirt

Solid waste

Scraper covers waste

198

Still other communities use large, modern *incinerators.* Solid wastes are burned in them at high temperature. Only a few ashes are left to be buried. And special devices help keep the incinerators from polluting the air.

In some large communities, garbage is burned in huge incinerators that turn heat to steam. This steam is used to make electricity. The electricity is used to heat and light the community.

What does your community do with solid wastes?

What do you and your family do to reduce your trash and garbage?

Sum It Up

In what ways can food be polluted?

How can housing be improved?

What are some healthy ways for communities to get rid of solid wastes?

Teacher's Notes

As pupils discuss the ways in which communities may dispose of solid wastes, jot their suggestions on the chalkboard. Later have students evaluate each method.

Discuss, too, how garbage and trash are disposed of in your community.

See also page T38 for additional teaching suggestions.

How is garbage changed into electricity for heating and lighting a community?

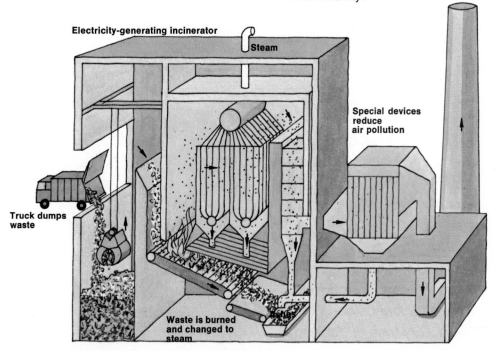

Electricity-generating incinerator

Steam

Special devices reduce air pollution

Truck dumps waste

Waste is burned and changed to steam

Ashes

What Can Be Done About Noise Pollution?

Noise is all around us. Cars honk. Brakes squeal. Sirens scream. And trucks rumble along the streets.

People also listen to loud noises in the home. TV sets, radios, and record players may be too loud. And the sound of vacuum cleaners, lawnmowers, and kitchen equipment add to the problem.

In some communities people work in noisy factories. At airports some workers hear the roar of airplanes all day long.

Scientists know that too much noise can be harmful to health. Noise can make some people nervous, disturb their sleep, or make them tire easily.

Sudden noise may make the heart beat faster. Blood vessels may get smaller, or contract. The pupils of the eyes may become larger.

Working in noisy places can make some people hard of hearing. And noise from rock bands can cause temporary loss of hearing.

200

Teacher's Notes
After studying page 201, discuss the effects of too much noise on people's health. You might ask why it is not a good idea to blow a horn or shout into another person's ear. (Loud noises sometimes injure the *eardrum*, a skinlike part that stretches across the *auditory canal* inside the ear.)
When discussing ways to reduce noise pollution, see what students know about such efforts in their own community. (Embankments along freeways, for example, might have been planted with shrubs or ivy to muffle some of the noise from vehicles. There might be parks in the community to provide quiet, restful places for people to enjoy.)
See also page T38 for additional teaching suggestions.

Books to Read

Look at the library for books about noise. Here are some good ones:
Hutchins, Carleen M. *Who Will Drown the Sound?* (Coward).
Perera, Thomas and Gretchen. *Louder and Louder: The Dangers of Noise Pollution* (Watts).

Some Ways to Reduce Noise

Many things can be done to cut down on noise. Special materials can be used to sound-proof buildings. These materials are put on walls, windows, and ceilings. They keep indoor noises from being carried from room to room. And they keep outdoor noises from coming inside.

Carpeting on the floors of homes, schools, and offices is a good way to reduce noise. We also know that trees, grass, and bushes help absorb noise.

Many communities have passed laws to keep car drivers from honking horns, except in emergencies. Other towns have laws that require noisy factories to close at night.

Today, many machines are made with motors less noisy than they once were. Some factories put noisy machines in soundproof rooms. Or workers may have to wear special earmuffs and earplugs.

Scientists are trying to learn how to reduce noise made by jet planes. One way is to put sound-absorbing material around the engines.

What are some noises that might disturb people in your community, your school, and your home?

What does your community do about noise control? Your school? What can you do to help?

Sum It Up

What are some "noise-makers" in your community?

How can too much loud noise affect people's health?

What are four ways to cut down on noise pollution in a community?

202

Things to Do

Teacher's Notes
Item 4: You might discuss what happens to old glass jars and bottles and to cans that are collected and recycled. (Glass can be ground up and used to make new glass. Cans can be melted down in large furnaces and eventually made into new cans.) Old newspapers, magazines, grocery bags, and other pieces of paper can also be collected and recycled. (Factories shred the papers and turn them into *pulp*. The pulp is used to make new paper.)
See also page T38 for additional teaching suggestions.

1. Look at the picture below. What has happened to spoil something in the community? How might the building be improved?

2. Find out what things your food store does to help keep the food clean and safe.

3. After studying about air pollution, one person said, "My family is going to walk places whenever we can. We're going to help cut down on air pollution by not riding everywhere in a car."

What do you think about this? Write your opinion on a piece of paper.

4. Bring to class examples of things made from *recycled* paper. Use the objects to make an exhibit.

5. Suppose you could plan some new homes for people in a large city. Your homes would replace old ones that had been torn down. Tell what plans you would make for safe and healthful homes. How might some of your plans apply to old houses?

Can You Show What You Know?[1]

Teacher's Notes
Here behavioral objectives in the *cognitive* area are posed in childlike language directly to the children themselves. In turn, boys and girls give evidence by *observable behavior* of what they have learned.
Other hoped-for behavioral objectives lie chiefly in the less easily observed *affective* area—objectives that pertain to feelings, attitudes, and values. Some of them are:
Develops some awareness of the health problems a community faces.
Assumes some responsibility for helping cut down on various kinds of pollution.
Participates in community recycling activities.

Page numbers show you where to look back in the chapter for information, if you need it.

1. Tell some things a community health department does. (177–179)

2. Explain how air may become polluted. (181)

3. Tell how air pollution can affect health. (182)

4. Mention two ways to reduce air pollution. (183)

5. Tell about some of the things a sewage-treatment plant does. (186)

6. Explain the main purpose of a water-treatment plant. (187)

7. Tell three ways to prevent food pollution. (189)

8. Describe one good way to dispose of solid wastes in a community. (198–199)

9. Suggest three ways in which noise can affect people's health. (201)

[1] Behavioral objectives in the cognitive area are stated here directly to students themselves.

Review It

Teacher's Notes
"Review It" is a feature that occurs at the end of each chapter in this book and in this health series. It gives children a chance to think over what they have learned, to summarize, and to store away important ideas. Page references after each item make this review page a self-help one. However, group discussion can be a valuable adjunct.

Page numbers show you where to look back in the chapter for information, if you need it.

1. When is a community likely to have smog settle over it? (182)

2. How would you explain this statement: "Air pollution is expensive"? (182)

3. In what ways can food become polluted? (189)

4. What are some important guides for food handlers? (190)

5. What are some disadvantages to a community when there is a polluted body of water nearby? (191)

6. Why is poor housing a community health problem? What can be done about poor housing? (193)

7. What can be done to cut down on noise around us? (202)

8. What is wrong with dumping garbage in open dumps? (198)

Copy each numbered item from List A. After each item, write the letter and words from List B that best describe it. For example:

9. emphysema   g. a disease of the lungs

List A

9. emphysema
10. incinerator
11. litter
12. pesticide
13. reservoir
14. sanitarian
15. solid wastes

List B

a. trash that is scattered about
b. furnace
c. garbage and trash
d. public health specialist
e. storage place for water
f. insect and weed killer
g. a disease of the lungs

Health Test for Chapter Seven

Teacher's Notes
After students have taken the test and their papers have been scored, the test items can serve as guides for a summary discussion. Volunteers can read aloud their rewording of the false statements.
(*Note:* "What Do You Think?" is a special feature that offers pupils a chance to evaluate some of their newly acquired knowledge.)

Copy each number on a piece of paper. After each number write the correct answer, *true* or *false.* Rewrite each false statement to make it true.

F 1. You can always see air that is polluted.

T 2. Air pollution can damage buildings and other property.

F 3. Smog is harmless.

T 4. Smoke can cause air pollution.

F 5. Garbage and other wastes should be burned in open dumps.

T 6. Trees and bushes help absorb noise.

T 7. Litter can be unsanitary.

T 8. Rivers and lakes can be polluted by having sewage dumped into them.

T 9. Water is treated at a water-treatment plant to make it safe for people to use.

F 10. Polluted waters are safe, pleasant places for swimming.

T 11. Germs in food can spread disease.

T 12. Loud noises can harm people's health.

T 13. Air pollution can irritate the eyes and nose.

T 14. Poor housing can be a community health problem.

F 15. Food handlers should touch the inside of cups and glasses.

T 16. Lakes and rivers may be polluted by sewage.

F 17. Foods that spoil easily should be kept in the cupboard.

F 18. Smog is most likely to occur on a windy day.

T 19. Air can be polluted by smoke and gas.

T 20. A health department has sanitarians.

Number of Answers   __20__

Number Right   _____

Score (Number Right × 5)   _____

What Do You Think?

What did you learn in this chapter that you think everyone should know? Write about it on another piece of paper.

SCHOOL & HOME

Teacher's Notes
Special efforts are made in this book and in this health series to foster school-home communication.
Here students have an opportunity to share with their families ideas about things they can do to cut down on air pollution, litter, noise, and trash.

You have learned things your community does to help cut down on pollution. But you and your family can also help. The quiz below may give you some ideas.

You might copy the quiz and take it home.

We're Not Polluters and Wasters (Or Are We?)

1. Do we go everywhere in the family ?

Or do we go by or by ?

2. When we ride in the car, do we throw trash out

the  ? Or do we put it in a ?

3. Do we keep the or turned

up loud? Or turned down just loud enough to hear?

4. Do we throw away almost every and

 ? Or do we save them to use again?

Do You *Use* What You Know?[1]

Teacher's Notes

This is an end-of-book review *with special emphasis on how children are applying their health and safety knowledge in daily life.* A notable feature of this review is the provision for children to look back to pages in the book that can tell them things they need to know, in case they have forgotten. The review should facilitate a transfer of important health and safety ideas from the book to everyday life.

Page numbers show you where to look back in the book for information, if you need it.

1. What interestng thing can you tell about someone in your group? (12–13)

2. What likeable thing have you done lately? (16)

3. Have you felt shy or scared lately? What did you do about your feelings? (18)

4. Have you felt angry lately? What did you do about your angry feelings? (20)

5. What have you done so far today to help keep yourself safe? (74, 76, 78, 80)

6. Have you driven a bike lately? If so, what did you do to be a safe bike driver? (76, 78)

7. Suppose you bruise or burn yourself. What will you do about it? (93)

8. What is one healthful thing you did this morning before coming to school? (101, 110, 138, 139)

9. How many hours of sleep did you get last night? Was it enough? (110)

10. What do you do to try and have healthy teeth? (138, 139, 142, 143)

11. What have you done lately to help keep from spreading disease germs? (155, 167, 189, 190)

12. What have you or your family done recently to help cut down on all kinds of pollution? (183, 190, 195, 197, 202)

---

[1] This is an end-of-book review, with emphasis on application of health and safety ideas in daily life. Numbers refer to pages where ideas being reviewed are presented.

Books for Boys and Girls[1]

Books of Information

Borghese, Anita. *The Down to Earth Cookbook* (Scribner).

Elliott, Sarah M. *Our Dirty Air* (Messner).

_____. *Our Dirty Water* (Messner).

Hammond, Winifred G. *The Riddle of Teeth* (Coward).

Lietz, Gerald S. *Bacteria.* A Junior Science Book (Garrard).

Perera, Thomas and Gretchen. *Louder and Louder: The Dangers of Noise Pollution* (Watts).

Ravielli, Anthony. *Wonders of the Human Body* (Viking).

Rinkoff, Barbara. *No Pushing, No Ducking: Safety in the Water* (Lothrop).

Shay, Arthur. *What It's Like to Be a Dentist* (Reilly & Lee).

_____. *What It's Like to Be a Doctor* (Reilly & Lee).

_____. *What It's Like to Be a Nurse* (Reilly & Lee).

Books to "Grow On"

Clymer, Eleanor. *My Brother Stevie* (Holt). An older sister worries about her younger brother getting into trouble.

Heide, Florence P. *The Key* (Atheneum). This book has three stories. In each story a child must deal with a difficult situation.

Rich, Louise D. *Star Island Boy* (Watts). Larry goes to live with another set of foster parents. This time he finds a real home.

Shotwell, Louisa R. *Roosevelt Grady* (World). The son of a migrant worker longs for a permanent home.

Speevack, Yetta. *The Spider Plant* (Atheneum). A girl from Puerto Rico adjusts to apartment-house living.

Stolz, Mary. *A Wonderful, Terrible Time* (Harper). Two city girls go to summer camp.

Warburg, Sandol S. *Growing Time* (Houghton). Jamie learns to deal with grief after his pet dog dies.

---

[1] See also page T39 for additional books.

METRIC MEASURES

CUSTOMARY MEASURES

LENGTH

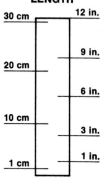

10 millimeters (mm)	= 1 centimeter (cm)
100 centimeters	= 1 meter (m)
1000 meters	= 1 kilometer (km)

12 inches (in.)	= 1 foot (ft.)
3 feet	= 1 yard (yd.)
5280 feet	= 1 mile (mi.)

MASS (WEIGHT)

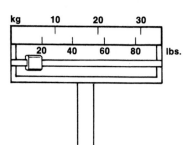

1000 milligrams (mg)	= 1 gram (g)
1000 grams	= 1 kilogram (kg)
1000 kilograms	= 1 metric ton (t)

| 16 ounces (oz.) | = 1 pound (lb.) |
| 2000 pounds | = 1 ton (t.) |

VOLUME

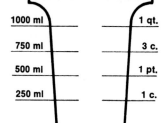

| 1000 milliliters (ml) | = 1 liter (l) |
| 1000 liters | = 1 kiloliter (kl) |

8 fluid ounces (fl. oz.)	= 1 cup (c.)
2 cups	= 1 pint (pt.)
2 pints	= 1 quart (qt.)
4 quarts	= 1 gallon (gal.)

TEMPERATURE

CELSIUS

FAHRENHEIT

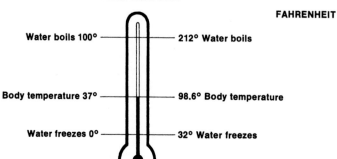

Water boils 100° — 212° Water boils

Body temperature 37° — 98.6° Body temperature

Water freezes 0° — 32° Water freezes

Glossary

This pronunciation key is adapted from the *Thorndike Barnhart Intermediate Dictionary*.

Full Pronunciation Key

The pronunciation of each word is shown just after the word, in this way: **ab bre vi ate** (ə brē′vē āt). The letters and signs used are pronounced as in the words at the right. The mark ′ is placed after a syllable with primary or heavy accent, as in the example above. The mark ′ after a syllable shows a secondary or lighter accent, as in **ab bre vi a tion** (ə brē′vē ā′shən).

Foreign Sound: H as in German ach. Pronounce k without closing the breath passage.

a	hat, cap	p	paper, cup
ā	age, face	r	run, try
ä	father, far	s	say, yes
		sh	she, rush
b	bad, rob	t	tell, it
ch	child, much	th	thin, both
d	did, red	ᴛʜ	then, smooth
e	let, best	u	cup, butter
ē	equal, be	u̇	full, put
ėr	term, learn	ü	rule, move
f	fat, if	v	very, save
g	go, bag	w	will, woman
h	he, how	y	young, yet
i	it, pin	z	zero, breeze
ī	ice, five	zh	measure, seizure
j	jam, enjoy	ə	represents:
k	kind, seek		a in about
l	land, coal		e in taken
m	me, am		i in pencil
n	no, in		o in lemon
ng	long, bring		u in circus
o	hot, rock	ər	represents
ō	open, go		er in mother
ô	order, all		ur in pursuit
oi	oil, voice		
ou	house, out		

211

ac id (as′id), 1. sour; sharp or biting to the taste: *Lemons are an acid fruit.* 2. a chemical substance. The acids caused by fermentation of sweet foods in the mouth can cause cavities. These foods can be removed by brushing the teeth.

al co hol (al′kə hôl), colorless liquid in gin, whiskey, wine, beer, etc., that makes them intoxicating; grain alcohol; ethyl alcohol.

an ti bi ot ic (an′ti bī ot′ik), substance produced by bacteria, yeast, and molds that destroys or weakens harmful microbes: *Penicillin is an antibiotic that kills harmful germs.*

an ti bod y (an′ti bod′ē), *pl.* **an ti bod ies,** substance produced in the blood or tissues of the body. It can destroy or weaken bacteria. Or it can make ineffective the poisons produced by bacteria.

ar ter y (är′tər ē), *pl.* **ar ter ies,** any of the blood vessels that carry blood away from the heart to all parts of the body.

back bone (bak′bōn′), the main bone along the middle of the back in humans and other mammals; the spine. The backbone is made up of many separate bones, called vertebrae.

bac ter i a (bak tir′ē ə), tiny living plants that can usually be seen only through a microscope. Some harmful bacteria cause disease or tooth decay. Some helpful bacteria turn milk into cheese or cider into vinegar.

bi cus pid (bī kus′pid), tooth having two cusps, or pointed ends, that tears and grinds food. An adult has eight bicuspids.

blood pres sure (blud′ presh′ər), pressure, or continued force, of the blood against the walls of the arteries: *Some people have abnormally high blood pressure.*

blood ves sel (blud′ ves′əl), any tube in the body through which the blood circulates. An artery, vein, or capillary is a blood vessel.

boost er dose (bü′stər dōs′), additional dose of a vaccine or serum given at stated intervals after the original dose. It may also be given as emergency treatment when exposure to a disease has occurred or is suspected.

brain (brān), a soft, spongy mass of nerve cells inside the skull or head of a person or animal. The brain controls almost all of the functions of the body. It enables us to learn, think, and remember.

bron chi tis (brong kī′tis), inflammation of the mucous membrane that lines the bronchial tubes in the lungs.

cal cu lus (kal′kyə ləs), *see* **tartar.**

can cer (kan′sər), harmful growth in the body that tends to spread and destroy healthy tissues and organs; malignant tumor.

car bon di ox ide (kär′bən dī ok′sīd), colorless, odorless gas present in air. It is a waste product formed by the body. It is removed from the body by the lungs. You breathe out, or exhale, carbon dioxide that is in your lungs.

cav i ty (kav′ə tē), *pl.* **cav i ties,** hole in a tooth; hollow place.

cell (sel), basic building block of living matter. Animals and plants are made of cells.

ce men tum (sə men′təm), bonelike tissue that covers the roots of teeth.

cold-blood ed (kōld′blud′id), having blood that is about as cold as the air or water around the animal. Reptiles are cold-blooded; birds and mammals are warm-blooded.

com mu ni ca ble dis ease (kə myü′nə kə-bəl də zēz′), disease which can be passed from person to person.

crown (kroun), part of a tooth that appears above the gum, or an artificial replacement for it.

cus pid (kus′pid), tooth having one cusp, or pointed end, used especially for tearing food. An adult has four cuspids.

den tal hy gien ist (den′tl hī′jē′nist), person who assists a dentist, especially in cleaning teeth.

den tin (den′tin), layer of hard, bony material beneath the enamel of a tooth. It forms the main part of a tooth.

di a be tes (dī′ə bē′tis or dī′ə bē′tēz), disease in which a person's body cannot use normal amounts of sugar and starch.

di gest (də jest′ or dī jest′), change (food) in the mouth, stomach, and intestines so that the body can use it.

diph ther i a (dif thir′ē ə or dip thir′ē ə), communicable disease of the nose and throat. You can be immunized against it.

dis ease (də zēz′), condition in which a body organ, system, or part does not work properly; sickness; illness.

drug (drug), substance used as a medicine or in preparing medicines. Drugs are obtained from plants, molds, minerals, and so on, and are often made from chemicals.

dys en ter y (dis′ən ter′ē), disease of the intestines, producing diarrhea with mucus and blood.

e lec tron mi cro scope (i lek′tron mī′krə-skōp), microscope that uses beams of electrons rather than beams of light to enlarge images. It has much higher power than an ordinary light microscope.

e mo tion (i mō′shən), strong feeling of any kind. Joy, grief, fear, hate, love, anger, and excitement are emotions.

em phy se ma (em′fə sē′mə), respiratory disease in which the air sacs of the lungs become enlarged. The air sacs are less able to supply oxygen to the blood and remove carbon dioxide from it.

e nam el (i nam′əl), the hard, white substance that covers and protects the crown of a tooth.

e soph a gus (ē sof′ə gəs), the tube for the passage of food from the mouth to the stomach.

floss (flôs), a soft, waxed or unwaxed thread used for cleaning between the teeth: *Use dental floss to clean between the teeth.*

---

a hat, ā age, ä far; e let, ē be, ėr term; i it, ī ice; o hot, ō go, ô order; oi oil, ou out; u cup, u̇ put, ü rule; ch child; ng long; sh she; th thin; ᴛH then; zh measure; ə taken, mother

flu o ride (flü′ə rīd′), substance that can help prevent tooth decay. It may be added to drinking water or toothpaste. It may be put directly on the teeth by a dentist.

gas (gas), substance that is not a solid or a liquid. It has no shape or size of its own and can expand without limit: *Oxygen is a gas.*

germ (jėrm), a very tiny animal, plant, or other living organism which is too small to be seen without a microscope; a microbe that causes disease.

gum (gum), the firm flesh around the teeth.

health (helth), 1. a being well or not sick; freedom from sickness. 2. condition of the body: *good health, poor health.*

heart (härt), hollow organ made of muscle. It pumps the blood throughout the body.

high blood pres sure, *see* **blood pressure.**

im mu ni ty (i myü′nə tē), one's protection from or resistance to disease.

im mu nize (im′yə nīz), protect from disease by inoculation or natural infection: *Vaccination can immunize a person against smallpox.*

in cin e ra tor (in sin′ə rā′tər), furnace for burning trash and other things.

in ci sor (in sī′zər), tooth having a sharp edge for cutting; one of the front teeth. An adult has eight incisors.

i ris (ī′ris), colored part of the eye around the pupil. Muscles in the iris control the size of the pupil.

kid ney (kid′nē), one of the pair of organs in the body that takes liquid wastes and excess water out of the blood. The kidneys then pass on these wastes, called *urine,* to the urinary bladder.

Klee, Paul (klā′ pôl′), 1879–1940, Swiss painter.

large in tes tine (lärj′ in tes′tən), the lower part of the intestines where water is absorbed and wastes are eliminated; large bowel.

liv er (liv′ər), large body organ that makes a digestive juice and helps the body use food. The liver also changes sugar into a different form and stores it.

lung (lung), one of a pair of saclike, spongy body organs located in the chest. When you breathe in, the lungs take oxygen from the air. When you breathe out, they release carbon dioxide into the air.

ma lar i a (mə ler′ē ə *or* mə lar′ē ə), disease that causes chills, fever, and sweating. It is caused by a protozoan. It is transmitted by the anopheles mosquito.

med i cine (med′ə sən), substance, such as a drug, used to treat, prevent, or cure disease; medication.

mem brane (mem′brān), thin, soft sheet or layer of animal tissue. It covers, separates, or connects some parts of the body.

mi crobe (mī′krōb), any kind of living thing that is too small to be seen except with a microscope: *Germs are microbes that cause disease.*

214

mi cro scope (mī′krə skōp), instrument with one or more lenses that make small things look larger: *Bacteria can only be seen through a microscope.*

mo lar (mō′lər), tooth with a broad surface for grinding. Your back teeth are molars.

mo tor nerve (mō′tər nėrv′), bundle of nerve fibers that carry messages from the brain or spinal cord to the muscles.

mu cus (myü′kəs), slimy substance that is made by and that moistens the linings of body cavities.

mus cle (mus′əl), tissue that can be shortened or lengthened to make the body move.

nerve (nėrv), fiber or bundle of fibers that carry messages between the brain or spinal cord and other parts of the body.

nerv ous sys tem (nėr′vəs sis′təm), body system made up of the brain, spinal cord, nerves, and other nervous tissue. The nervous system receives and sends messages.

non com mu ni ca ble dis ease (non′kə-myü′nə kə bəl də zēz′), disease that is not caused by germs and that cannot be passed from one person to another. It is usually caused by some problem within the body.

or gan (ôr′gən), any group of tissues in the body that work together to perform one or more special jobs. The eyes, stomach, and lungs are all organs.

or tho don tist (ôr′thə don′tist), dentist who specializes in aligning teeth or moving them into proper position.

ox y gen (ok′sə jen), colorless, odorless gas that is needed by many living things. It is taken into the body by breathing in.

pace mak er (pās′mā′kər), 1. special tissue in the heart that sends out impulses. These impulses keep the heart beating at a normal rhythm. 2. an artificial device placed inside a person's chest to maintain or restore the normal rhythm of the heart.

pe des tri an (pə des′trē ən), a person who goes on foot: *Pedestrians have to watch for automobiles turning corners.*

per i o don tal mem brane (per′ē ə don′tl mem′brān), elastic fibers that line the tooth socket below the gum. The membrane holds the tooth in place in the jaw.

per ma nent teeth (pėr′mə nənt tēth′), the second set of teeth (of which there are 32), which start to come in when the primary teeth begin to come out. They are intended to last a lifetime.

per spi ra tion (pėr′spə rā′shən), sweat: *The runner's forehead was damp with perspiration.*

pes ti cide (pes′tə sīd), substance used to kill pests such as insects and weeds.

pig ment (pig′mənt), substance that occurs in and colors the tissues of an animal or plant. The color of a person's hair or skin is due to pigment in the body cells.

---

a hat, ā age, ä far; e let, ē be, ėr term; i it, ī ice; o hot, ō go, ô order; oi oil, ou out; u cup, u̇ put, ü rule; ch child; ng long; sh she; th thin; ᵺH then; zh measure; ə taken, mother

plaque (plak), thin film composed of saliva, bacteria, and food debris. It is constantly being formed on the surfaces of the teeth.

po li o (pō′lē ō), communicable disease caused by a virus. It destroys tissue in the spinal cord and can cause crippling and death. There are vaccines that can prevent polio.

pol lute (pə lüt′), make dirty, unclean, or impure: *The water at the beach was polluted by sewage from the city.*

pol lu tion (pə lü′shən), addition of manmade products to the environment which can be a danger to the health and survival of living things.

pre scrip tion (pri skrip′shən), written direction or order for preparing and using a medicine.

pro to zo an (prō′tə zō′ən), one of a group of microscopic animals that are single cells. Some protozoans cause disease.

pulp (pulp), soft, inner part of a tooth, containing blood vessels and nerves.

pulse (puls), regular beating of the arteries, caused each time the heart contracts. The arteries get larger as the heart contracts and forces more blood into them. The arteries get smaller as the heart relaxes.

pu pil (pyü′pəl), opening in the center of the iris of the eye. The pupil becomes larger or smaller to let more or less light into the eye. It looks like a black spot.

re cy cle (rē sī′kəl), to process or treat something so that it may be used again.

res er voir (rez′ər vwär), place where water is collected and stored for later use.

root (rüt *or* ruṫ), part of a tooth that is covered by the gums and cannot be seen. It holds the tooth in position in the jaw.

sa li va (sə lī′və), liquid that the salivary glands make and then empty into the mouth. It keeps the mouth moist, helps in chewing, and starts digestion of food.

sal i var y gland (sal′ə ver′ē gland′), any of the glands in the mouth that produce saliva.

san i tar i an (san′ə ter′ē ən), worker in sanitary science and public health: *Sanitarians inspect milk and food.*

san i tar y (san′ə ter′ē), 1. favorable to health; preventing disease. 2. free from dirt and filth.

san i tar y land fill (san′ə ter′ē land′fil′), method of garbage disposal. Garbage is buried and covered over with fresh earth.

sca ler (skā′lər), instrument for removing tartar, or calculus, from the teeth.

sem i cir cu lar ca nal (sem′i sėr′kyə lər kə nal′), any of the three curved, tubelike canals in the inner ear that help us keep our balance.

sen sor y nerve (sen′sər ē nėrv′), bundle of nerve fibers that carry messages from the sense organs to the brain or spinal cord. Some of these messages are pain, temperature, touch, sight, smell, sound, and taste.

sew age (sü′ij), waste water and rubbish that pass through underground pipes.

skel e tal mus cles (skel ə təl mus′əlz), muscles that are attached to the bones of the body.

skull (skul), bony framework of the head and face. It encloses and protects the brain.

sleep ing sick ness (slē′ping sik′nis), disease causing fever, weakness, loss of weight, sleepiness, and usually death. It is caused by a protozoan and is common in Africa.

smog (smog), combination of smoke and fog in the air.

sol id waste (sol′id wāst′), rubbish or trash, which consists of cartons, cans, crockery, glass, ashes, old clothing, and so on; also garbage, which is waste resulting from growing, preparing, cooking, and serving food.

spi nal cord (spī nəl kôrd), thick, whitish cord of nerve tissue that extends from the brain down through most of the backbone. Nerves go from the spinal cord to different parts of the body.

tar tar (tär′tər), hard substance formed by the action of saliva on food; calculus. It collects on the teeth and is removed by a dentist.

tis sue (tish′ü), living substance that forms some part of an animal or plant; a mass of similar cells that performs a particular function: *muscle tissue, nerve tissue.*

tooth de cay (tüth′ di kā′), destruction of dental tissues; rotting of a tooth; cavity; dental caries.

ur i nar y blad der (yur′ə ner′ē blad′ər), soft, thin sac in the body that receives urine from the kidneys. The bladder stores and later discharges urine.

vac cine (vak′sēn′ *or* vak sēn′), substance containing weakened or killed viruses or bacteria of a certain disease. When injected into the body or given orally, vaccines cause the body to produce antibodies.

vein (vān), any of the blood vessels that carry blood to the heart from all parts of the body.

vi rus (vī′rəs), one of a group of microbes that produce disease. They can only be seen through an electron microscope. Viruses cause diseases such as polio.

white blood cells (hwīt′ blud′ selz′), colorless cells that float in the blood and lymph. Some of them destroy disease germs.

whoop ing cough (hüp′ing kôf′), communicable disease that causes fits of coughing that end with a loud, gasping sound. It is caused by a type of bacteria.

wind pipe (wind′pīp′), passage by which air is carried from the throat to the lungs; the trachea.

---

a hat, **ā** age, **ä** far; **e** let, **ē** be, **ėr** term; **i** it, **ī** ice; **o** hot, **ō** go, **ô** order; **oi** oil, **ou** out; **u** cup, **u̇** put, **ü** rule; **ch** child; **ng** long; **sh** she; **th** thin; **ŦH** then; **zh** measure; **ə** taken, mother

Index

218

About the Book

This book is a part of the Scott, Foresman Health series. It grows out of the preceding popular *Health and Growth* series which has already been used by several million children. Learner and teacher feedback on *Health and Growth* has pointed the way to this new highly teachable series.

This book has high interest for children in the "middle school" years. It is of particular interest to pupils from nine- to ten-years-old or so. Research on the needs, concerns, curiosities, and interests of this age group are taken into account in the book.

Children of this age have special personal and social needs. They have concern about having friends, being liked, feeling good about themselves, and learning to deal with shy, scared, or angry feelings.

Youngsters from nine- to ten-years-old or thereabouts ask more questions about germs and diseases than about any other topic.[1] These children are also interested in foods—how to prepare them and why we need them. They are fascinated by the wonders of the body. Teeth are a high-interest topic, too.

Interests and concerns are expanding to include community, or environmental, health.

Safety needs revolve chiefly around pedestrian safety, bicycle safety, safety around water, falls, and safety with drugs.

Interspersed throughout each chapter are special features such as health-related poems and works of art and children's own writings on pertinent health topics. And a notable feature of each chapter ending is the "School & Home" page which motivates sharing health information at home and applying it in daily living.

Tests and quick reviews abound and help pupils check their own progress.

Marginal notes to pupils and "Things to Do" sections at chapter endings also offer a variety of activities, reading lists, demonstrations, and experiments.

To facilitate successful use of this book by the children for whom it is particularly intended, much attention has been given to making the text highly readable.

---

[1] *Teach Us What We Want to Know* by Ruth Byler, Gertrude Lewis, and Ruth Totman. Published for The Connecticut Board of Education, by The Mental Health Materials Center, 419 Park Avenue South, New York, New York 10016.

Acknowledgments

For illustrations and photographs on these pages:
Cover—Mike Mauney. 39—Photographs from Federal
Bureau of Investigation, U.S. Department of Justice,
Washington, D.C. 41—Copyright © 1972, 1974 by Scott,
Foresman and Company. 43—Courtesy David R. Watts,
M.D. 46–49—Copyright © 1971, 1974 by Scott, Foresman
and Company. 50—Scala, New York/Florence. 53—
Copyright © 1972, 1974 by Scott, Foresman and Com-
pany. 55, 57–64, 76, 79, 81–85, 88, 111, 116–117—
Copyright © 1971, 1974 by Scott, Foresman and Com-
pany. 118–121—Adaptation of Nancy Bayley's Growth
Charts (Information on Child Growth Patterns) from *The
New Encyclopedia of Child Care and Guidance,* edited
by Sidonie Matsner Gruenberg. Copyright © 1954, 1956,
1959, 1963, 1968 by Doubleday & Company, Inc. Repro-
duced by permission of Doubleday & Company, Inc.
131–137, 140—Copyright © 1971, 1974 by Scott, Fores-
man and Company. 141—Photographs from Captain
Gordon H. Rovelstad, United States Navy, Naval Dental
Research Institute, Naval Training Center, Great Lakes,
Illinois. 142–143—Copyright © 1971, 1974 by Scott,
Foresman and Company. 144—Scala, New York/
Florence. 156, 157 (Top), 159—Courtesy Dr. Leon J.
LeBeau, Department of Microbiology, University of
Illinois at the Medical Center, Chicago, Illinois. 157 (Bot-
tom Left, Bottom Right)—Photographs courtesy of Clay
Adams, Division of Becton, Dickinson and Company,
Parsippany, New Jersey. 158 (Top)—Courtesy A. R.
Taylor, Ph.D., Laboratory Director—Virus Research,
Parke, Davis & Co. 158 (Bottom Left)—Courtesy of the
American Society for Microbiology. 158 (Bottom Right)—
Courtesy of the Virus Laboratory, University of Califor-
nia, Berkeley, California. 160—Courtesy Dr. James G.
Hirsch, The Rockefeller University. 162, 163, 178, 179
(Bottom Left)—Copyright © 1971, 1974 by Scott, Fores-
man and Company. 180–181—Copyright © 1974 by
Scott, Foresman and Company. 182—Copyright © 1971,
1974 by Scott, Foresman and Company. 184–185—John
Launois from Black Star. 186–187—Copyright © 1971,
1974 by Scott, Foresman and Company. 191—J. Collier
from Black Star. 200–201—Copyright © 1974 by Scott,
Foresman and Company.

224